GCSE
In a Week

English
Language & Literature

Ian
Kirby

Revision Planner

Unseen Non-Fiction

DAY 1

Unseen Fiction

DAY 2

Writing

DAY 3

Note: If you want to extend your preparation beyond the seven-day revision programme provided, opportunities for extra practice are labelled with this symbol EXTRA PRACTICE

General and Poetry

Shakespeare

19th Century Prose

20th Century Texts

Finding Information

You need to be able to find information about a specific aspect of a text, such as **facts**, **opinions**, or themes.

Finding Facts

If you are asked to identify facts, look for things that can be proven.

To help you, focus on finding:
- **statistics**
- proper nouns (names of people and places).

Example

My dad loved butterflies more than anything else. He had collected <u>112 different species</u>, including the beautiful <u>Blue Morpho</u>. This was his most impressive find as it came from deep in the forests of <u>Central America</u>.

Statistic

Proper Noun

Proper Noun

You could write:
One fact is that her dad had collected 112 species of butterfly. We are also told the name of a butterfly (Blue Morpho) and where it comes from (Central America).

If you have been given a specific theme to explore (such as 'daily routines' in a text about the army), make sure you stick to it.

Finding Opinions

Unlike facts, opinions cannot be proven: they are things that people think or feel.

For example: 'Spiders can be poisonous' is a fact but 'spiders are horrible' is an opinion (as other people might disagree).

To help you, focus on finding:
- judgement **adjectives** (like 'wonderful', 'terrible', 'tasty')
- speech marks (which might indicate someone sharing their opinions).

Finding Information on a Theme

You may also need to find information relating to a specific theme (for example, 'the weather' in a text about British summertime).

Being able to scan a text is a useful skill.
- Start by looking for the specific theme-word that you have been given. For example, this could be 'weather'.
- Also look for things that are related to the theme-word, in this case sun, fog, clouds, etc.

Example

Whenever we went on holiday, we went to the Lake District. Fresh air, beautiful rolling hills, crystal clear lakes, and <u>terrible weather</u>. I hated how it <u>poured with rain</u> every day. The <u>wind would whip</u> down from the mountain, biting at our skin and bringing with it <u>sub-zero temperatures</u>. How I longed for a beach in Spain like my best friend, Susan.

You could write:
We are told that the weather was terrible. The writer describes hating the pouring rain, along with the biting winds and sub-zero temperatures coming from the mountains.

Supporting Your Ideas With Quotations

If the exam question asks for evidence, you should put your ideas in your own words and support each one with a brief quotation from the text.

You can embed your quotation in your **sentence** by using different punctuation, such as a colon, a comma, or parentheses.

Example

We are told that the climate in the Lake District was awful: "terrible weather". The writer describes disliking the constant rainfall, "I hated how it poured with rain every day". As well as this, the mountain winds were painful ("biting at our skin") and freezing cold ("sub-zero temperatures").

Notice the use of synonyms so the student's words aren't just the same as those in the quotations, for example awful/terrible, freezing/sub-zero, etc. This shows that they understand the text.

Read this extract before attempting the Exam Practice questions.

In this extract from her autobiography, novelist Fay Weldon describes her childhood in Christchurch, New Zealand. Her parents have gone away, so she and her sister have been sent to a private hotel to be looked after by family friends.

Cranmer Square was not actually square but an oblong, its grass intersected by paths in the pattern of the Union Jack. In this city of boxy bungalows set in neat gardens it seemed to me a significant place, if sloppily named. Nearly all the buildings which lined it had stairs: that is to say they were more than one storey high. There was the Girls' High School at the north end, and St Margaret's to the west and the Normal School to the south. In between were boarding-houses and hotels. On wet days, when heavy rain drummed on the ground and made the corrugated-iron roofs rattle, slugs and snails would come out in enormous number to cover the stripes of the Union Jack, making walking hazardous. The crack of a snail beneath the shoe or the sight of a squashed worm strikes horror into the little-girl heart. There were few wet days, of course; winter in Christchurch was an eight-week affair and then it was over. The nor'wester* was a worse affliction*; wake up to see the arch of cloud in a heavy sky, and know that within hours the hard, hot, strong wind would get up and blow for days, making everyone cross and tired.

Jane and I shared a high damp steamy bed in the front ground-floor room. The bedspread was made of bright green artificial silk which was chilly and slippery to the touch. I cried a little on the first night we slept in it, and was proud of Jane, who didn't cry at all. There wasn't a pot under the bed and we didn't know where the lavatory was, so that night Jane wee-ed on the round Chinese carpet.

(from *Auto da Fay*, by Fay Weldon)

*nor'wester = the wind coming from the north-west
*affliction = a source of pain or misery

SUMMARY

- Facts can be proven using evidence.
- Opinions are simply what someone thinks or feels.
- When retrieving information, scan a text to find key words.
- When using quotations as evidence, you should write your ideas in your own words.

QUESTIONS

QUICK TEST

1. Which of these statements is a fact and which is an opinion?

   a. That tree is huge.   **b.** That's an oak tree.

2. What words might you scan for if you were searching a text about information on nature?

3. Why do you need to put ideas in your own words when using quotations as evidence?

EXAM PRACTICE

1. Find three facts about Cranmer Square. [3 marks]

2. Find three things Fay didn't like about living in Cranmer Square.   [3 marks]

3. Pick out the three statements about the text that are true.   [3 marks]

   i. Cranmer Square is actually oblong-shaped.

   ii. There is only one school.

   iii. It rains continually.

   iv. Jane and Fay have to share a bed.

   v. The bedspread is bright red.

   vi. Fay cries a little on the first night.

4. Using evidence, what do you learn about the weather in Christchurch, New Zealand? [6 marks]

Language and Structure: Thoughts and Feelings

You need to be able to analyse how a writer uses language and **structure** to show what they, or someone else, are thinking or feeling.

Focus

Read the exam question carefully.

Check whether you are focussing on general thoughts and feelings (for example: How does the writer show his different feelings during the journey?), or a specific emotion or idea (such as: How does the writer present his unhappiness?).

Vocabulary of Thought and Feelings

To help you explain your ideas, try to learn synonyms (and the different subtleties of their meanings) for different emotions.

For example:
- Happy – cheerful, joyous, exuberant, jolly, pleased
- Sad – miserable, depressed, melancholy, heartbroken, pessimistic
- Surprised – bewildered, astonished, shocked, awed.

Language

If you are asked to explore how language has presented thought or feeling, you need to analyse specific words, phrases and language techniques. (You can revise these areas on pages 48–49.)

Try to use the correct terminology.

Think about the **effect** of powerful **verbs**, adjectives, **adverbs**, **similes**, **metaphors**, etc.
- Find an example of the thought or feeling.
- Select a good quotation.
- Analyse how language has been used to show the thought or feeling.

Sample Question: How does the writer present his unhappiness?

Sunday, 10 April
Back pain continues! I'll have to ring Johnny Johnson tomorrow. It is murder… Woke at 5 o'c. Up at 7 o'c. Got papers. My spirits are so low. Everything conspires to make life intolerable.

(from *The Kenneth Williams Diaries*)

You might write:
The writer shows his unhappiness with: 'It is murder.' This metaphor uses a reference to killing to suggest the back pain is extreme and is destroying his life.

Structure

If you are asked to explore structure, consider two areas:
- Narrative structure – how the whole text shows the thought or feeling. Does it build up, stay the same, **develop**, or get resolved, etc.? How is this achieved?
- Sentence structure – how sentence lengths, sentence types and punctuation are used to **emphasise** thoughts or feelings.

(You can revise these areas on pages 50–51.)

Example
You could add to the previous analysis:
The narrative structure emphasises his misery. The series of short sentences build up a picture of his back problems. Then the final, longer sentence summarises how this pain is completely ruining his life.

Or:
Sentence structure is used to emphasise his misery, 'Back pain continues!' The short sentence stands out, indicating the pain is significantly affecting his life, and the exclamation mark suggests a cry of agony.

Read this extract before attempting the Exam Practice questions.

In this extract from his diaries, the actor Kenneth Williams describes his Saturday afternoon.

Saturday, 10 October

I was in good spirits & set out in the raincoat, walking to Selfridges where I got prawns for Louie. Back by 3 o'c marvellously cheerful & that insidious* voice inside began: 'Careful! Something will occur! Something will destroy all that elation before long!' Then I went in to see Louie & the TV news showed the horrible results of an IRA bomb outside Chelsea Barracks… a surgeon at the Westminster says the injuries are the worst he has ever seen. These heinous* crimes – in the name of *politics!* – go on, year in & year out… invalids live on, mutilated, blind, limbless… and the news shifts from this to the funeral today of the murdered Sadat of Egypt, and then: 'and now news of football…' etc. The misery welled up inside me & the spirits sank to zero.

(from *The Kenneth Williams Diaries*)

*insidious = causing harm in a gradual, initially unnoticed, way
*heinous = extremely bad

SUMMARY

- Read the question carefully to clarify your focus.
- Language = words, phrases, images.
- Structure = how a text builds up and the features of a sentence.
- Use correct terminology and explain how thoughts or feelings are shown.

QUESTIONS

QUICK TEST

1. How does the adjective help to show the writer's thoughts?
   The train journey took an exhausting nine hours.

2. How does the adverb help to show the writer's feelings?
   Despite my fears, the party was surprisingly fun.

3. How does the simile help to show the writer's nervousness?
   Waiting for the job interview, I felt like butterflies were hatching and fluttering around inside my stomach.

EXAM PRACTICE

Spend about 5 minutes reading the extract, then 15 minutes answering the questions.

1. a. Identify one phrase that shows Williams's happiness. [1 mark]

   b. Explain how your chosen phrase shows his happiness. [1 mark]

2. How does the writer use language to show his feelings? [6 marks]

3. How does the writer use structure to show his feelings? [6 marks]

Language and Structure: Engagement

Writers try to engage the reader by being interesting, entertaining, thought-provoking, funny, etc. You need to be able to analyse how they achieve engagement through their choices of language and structure.

Focus

Read the task carefully. Is it about engagement in general or does it specify something like entertaining or thought-provoking?

Words and Images

Start by looking for interesting or powerful uses of language.

Example

Lift the lid of a biscuit tin and you enter a world of chocolate Bourbons, understated, knobbly Lincolns, crumbly digestives and Jammie Dodgers. A secret place where there are lemon puffs, gingernuts, Jaffa Cakes and, if you are lucky, the occasional chocolate finger. No other country whose grocers' shelves I have encountered offers the punter and his purse such a display of sugar-sprinkled flour and butter, blobs of jam and drizzles of chocolate, crème fillings and white icing. We are the everyday biscuit capital of the world… What France is to cheese and Italy is to pasta, Britain is to the biscuit. The tin, with its tight lid and cute pictures, is a playground for those who like their snacks sweet and crisp and reeking of tradition.
    But there is more to it than that.

(from *Eating For England*, by Nigel Slater)

Metaphors	Adjectives
Nouns and noun phrases	Verbs

When you have identified a particular feature that is making the text effective, pick your best quotations and analyse their effect. Then analyse a different feature. By writing about different features separately, you are highlighting your understanding to the examiner.

Sample Question: How does Nigel Slater engage the reader with his use of language and structure?

You might write:
*Nigel Slater uses lots of adjectives to get us thinking about how tasty biscuits are: 'knobbly… crumbly… sweet… crisp'. By using different **senses** – like taste, smell, and touch – he gets us to imagine the pleasure of eating biscuits and this makes the writing pleasurable to read.*

He uses different noun phrases to create a similar effect. For example…

Register

Register means how simple or difficult the words are, and how **formal** or informal the writing is. For example, Nigel Slater uses the **second person** ('you') to address the reader. This is engaging because it makes us feel part of what is written.

He also uses familiar words (like Jaffa Cake) so we can relate to what he's describing, and colloquial words (such as 'punter') so it's like being chatted to by a friend.

Structure

Look for different features of sentence structure or narrative structure. For example, Nigel Slater has used **lists**, long sentences, short sentences, contrasts and cliffhangers. Don't just pick out the feature: analyse how it makes the writing engaging.

Example

You could add to the previous analysis:

The writer uses lists to build up images of biscuits. For example, 'lemon puffs, gingernuts, Jaffa Cakes'. These get us thinking about all the different biscuits that we like so we interact with the writer's opinions.

Read this extract before attempting the Exam Practice questions.

Toblerone

I have always found a bar of Toblerone almost as difficult to conquer as the mountain peaks its design so clearly represents. But beyond the familiar rattle of the bar in its triangular box, and the ragged job you inevitably make of unwrapping it from its foil, lies a quietly classic piece of confectionery quite unlike any other.

Whatever way you try to tackle it, a Toblerone is an obstacle course. It can take a few attempts to break a triangle from the nougat-speckled bar without actually hurting your knuckles, and then, when you finally do, you have a piece of pointy chocolate slightly too big for your mouth. You bite with your front teeth and find the chocolate barely gives, so you attempt to snap it with your fingers, and find that doesn't work either. The only thing left is to pop the whole lump in your mouth and suck.

The pointed end hits the roof of your mouth, so you roll it over with your tongue, only to find that it makes a lump in your cheek. It is as impossible to eat elegantly as a head of sweetcorn. The only answer is to let the nut-freckled chocolate soften slowly in the warmth of your mouth while rolling it over and over on your tongue. The nutty, creamy chocolate suddenly seems worth every bit of discomfort, and you decide to do it all over again with another piece.

We persevere because we think we like it, which of course we do, but there is more to it than that. Toblerone is a natural step between the cheap, fatty bars in purple wrapping and the posh stuff with its crispness and deep flavour further up the chocolate ladder. Any child who chooses the pyramid of mountain peaks over a slab of Dairy Milk is obviously on his or her way to becoming a chocolate connoisseur.

(from *Eating For England*, by Nigel Slater)

SUMMARY

- Be clear about the way the text is engaging: is it interesting, thought-provoking, funny, sad, surprising, etc? Or a combination of things?

- Analyse how specific features of language and structure create engaging effects.

- Separate your different language features rather than jumbling them up.

QUESTIONS

QUICK TEST

1. What is the effect of the short sentence?
   I have so many happy memories of my childhood, from climbing hills and canoeing down rivers to exploring caves and investigating rockpools. Everything was wonderful.

2. What feature of sentence structure can you see below and what is its effect?
   When you look around at all the pollution and waste in the world, don't you ever wonder how you could change the world for the better?

3. What feature of sentence structure can you see below and what is its effect?
   I was overwhelmed by the shopping centre, packed with people, prams, bright colours, glaring lights, posters and adverts.

EXAM PRACTICE

Spend about 5 minutes reading the extract, then 20 minutes answering the questions.

1. Explain one way in which Nigel Slater uses language to entertain in the first paragraph of 'Toblerone'. [3 marks]

2. Explain one way in which Nigel Slater uses structure to keep his audience reading in the first paragraph of 'Toblerone'. [3 marks]

3. How does Nigel Slater use language and structure to engage the reader in 'Toblerone'? [12 marks]

Comparing Texts: Summarising Similarities and Differences

You need to be able to select information that shows you understand the similarities and/or differences between the subjects of two texts.

State and Evidence

A typical exam question will ask you about the similarities and differences between the writers of two texts or the people they are describing. You are not being asked to analyse, just to retrieve comparative information. State your ideas in your own words and then support them with quotations.

Things to Look For

The question may be specific (for example: Find similarities about the writers' home lives). However, if the question is quite general, you need to scan the texts for possible information about gender, age, appearance, background, friends and family, job, feelings, behaviour, interests, etc.

How to Plan Your Response

You don't have much time so the most useful way to find your similarities and/or differences is to underline the text using different colours (one for each idea), or to note your ideas down using a Venn diagram.

Comparison Phrases

To join your ideas and make it clear that you are comparing, learn some of the following words and phrases:

- ● similarly; just as; the same; alike; equally; in common; likewise
- ● in contrast; however; whereas; is different; unlike; as opposed to; on the other hand

---

Example
What similarities and differences can you find in the writers' memories of authority figures?

Text A
My first <u>teacher</u> was an <u>aggressive</u> monster who <u>terrified me</u>. <u>Less than five feet tall</u>, he would creep between the desks in his <u>tatty tweed suit</u> and <u>hiss at us for not being clever enough</u>.

Text B
The <u>policeman</u> <u>towered above me: almost seven feet</u> from his <u>shiny boots to his polished helmet</u>. <u>His voice boomed</u> at me and <u>I froze completely</u>. But then I was surprised by how <u>gentle</u> he was when actually arresting me.

You might write:
Both figures of authority are scary. In Text A, the writer was 'terrified' by the teacher and, similarly, in Text B the writer says he 'froze completely' at the frightening sound of the policeman's voice.

However, the two men are physically different…

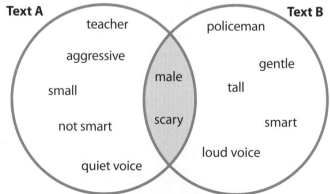

Text A: teacher, aggressive, small, not smart, quiet voice
Shared (male, scary)
Text B: policeman, gentle, tall, smart, loud voice

Read these extracts before attempting the Exam Practice questions.

Text A

My mother's childhood and girlhood were spent doing well in everything, because she had to please her stern father. She excelled in school, she played hockey and tennis and lacrosse well, she bicycled, she went to the theatre and music hall and musical evenings. Her energy was phenomenal. And she read all kinds of advanced books, and was determined her children would not have the cold and arid* upbringing she did…

Then she became a nurse, and had to live on the pay, which was so little she was often hungry and could not buy herself gloves and handkerchiefs or a nice blouse. The World War started, the first one, and my badly wounded father arrived in the ward where she was Sister McVeagh. He was there for over a year, and during that time her heart was well and truly broken, for the young doctor she loved and who loved her was drowned in a ship sunk by a torpedo.

(from *Under My Skin*, by Doris Lessing)

Text B

We have a young lady visitor with us – oh, mam, I wish you could be with us to see what the higher education of women leads to – she is 19 – a bursar* of Trinity College, first of her year in the hardest exam open to women – and such an addle-headed* womanly fool, to put it mildly, I never saw, so help me Bob. She knows the dates of all the Egyptian kings but she hasn't a word to say at the dinner table – she'll give you chapter and verse for any quotation but she has about as much poetry in her as a cow. She has the theory of music at her finger ends, and she won't play the accompaniment to a song – Lawn Tennis is too trivial* for her – she does not play games of chance – chess she plays. Dancing is childish – you never saw such an educated cabbage in your life.

(Letter to Amy Hoare, July 1881, from *Arthur Conan Doyle: A Life In Letters*)

*arid = dry and empty, like a desert
*a bursar = a student given financial aid so they can attend university
*addle-headed = stupid
*trivial = silly

SUMMARY

- Make sure you are clear about whether the question is asking for similarities, differences, or both.

- Put your ideas in your own words and support them with quotations.

- You are only finding and supporting points with evidence, not analysing the effects of language and structure.

QUESTIONS

QUICK TEST

1. When comparing people who have been written about in a text, what sort of things might you look for?

2. What techniques can you use to help you plan and order your response?

3. Give two phrases that suggest similarity and two phrases that suggest difference.

EXAM PRACTICE

Text A is an extract from Doris Lessing's autobiography, published in 1994, which describes her mother.

Text B is an extract from a letter, written by Arthur Conan Doyle in 1881, about his time as a medical student.

Spend about 5 minutes reading the two extracts, then 15 minutes answering the questions.

1. Find three similarities between the two women described in Texts A and B. [6 marks]

2. Find three differences between the two women described in Texts A and B. [6 marks]

Comparing Texts: How Ideas and Attitudes are Conveyed

You need to be able to analyse the similarities and differences in how two texts get across thoughts or feelings.

Preparing Your Answer

Start by making sure you know the focus of the question. It could be ideas and attitudes about the writers' places of work, or people they know, or places they have been to, etc.

Identify what each writer thinks and feels about the topic (and where this is shown in the text). Organise these ideas into points of similarity or difference.

Analysing

Whereas the summarising question asks you what you can find out about a text, this question is asking you how meaning is conveyed. You need clear analysis of language and structure.

Consider the effect of specific words and phrases, and the effects of sentence structure and narrative structure.

Sample Question: How do the two writers show their feelings about their babies?

Text A

March 1889

Baby is quite good at night, but we will be giving her a little sago & milk tonight as you advise. She is very fat & strong & laughs a great deal, especially when she looks at me. There is something about my appearance that strikes her as irresistibly funny.

(from *Arthur Conan Doyle: A Life In Letters*)

Text B

John at these tea parties did not behave badly; he was simply himself. Mary would say tartly, 'He's very energetic, isn't he?' watching him strive and wrestle in my arms, already putting his full weight on his feet…

I felt proud of John but abashed. I did not know why other people's babies lay calmly in their prams and allowed themselves to be dandled and cuddled.

(from *Under My Skin*, by Doris Lessing)

Possible ideas:
- Pleased/proud of baby
- Want baby to be calmer
- Impressed by baby's strength/ energy
- CD seems more distant (doesn't use the baby's name) than DL (perhaps due to traditional behaviour of men in the 19th century)
- CD enjoys his bond with his daughter but DL wishes her son was more like other babies.

Sample comparison and analysis:
Both writers are pleased with their babies. Conan Doyle is fairly happy with how the baby sleeps, 'quite good at night'. The use of the adjective 'good' shows he is praising her. Similarly, Lessing shows she is pleased with her son, 'I felt proud of John'. Like Conan Doyle, she uses an adjective ('proud') to show her positive feelings about her baby.

However, both parents want their baby to be calmer…

Notice the **paragraph** begins with a **topic sentence** of comparison. Then there is a point about Text A, a relevant quotation, and analysis of a specific feature. A connective then links the points and compares. This is followed by a point about Text B, a relevant quotation, analysis of specific features and some specific comparison with Text A.

Read these extracts before attempting the Exam Practice questions.

Text C

July 5, 1890

I have finished my great labour, & The White Company has come to an end. The first half is very good, the next quarter is pretty good, the last quarter very good again, and it ends with the true heroic note. Rejoice with me, dear, for I am as fond of Hordle John, and Samkin Aylward and Sir Nigel Loring [*the three main characters in the novel*], as though I knew them in the flesh, and I feel that the whole English speaking race will come in time to be so also.

(from *Arthur Conan Doyle: A Life In Letters*)

Text D

I remember the feeling of exaltation as I wrote those two satisfactory words, 'The End'. This was my métier*. This was what I was meant to do. This was what I had been born for. This I would do to the end of my days, and there was so much unsaid in the world I could go on saying it for ever.

But looking through *The Fat Woman's Joke*, now so proudly published, Louis Simpson merely groaned. He said this was simply not how novel writing was done. I had a terrible feeling he was right… It had all been a terrible, humiliating mistake.

(from *Mantrapped*, by Fay Weldon)

*métier = occupation or profession

SUMMARY

- Look for similar and different ideas in the two texts.
- Support them with relevant quotations.
- Analyse how the ideas are conveyed through language and structure.
- Use connectives to link your ideas.

QUESTIONS

QUICK TEST

1. What is the difference between a 'How…' exam question and a 'What…' exam question?

2. What should you use to link your ideas and show that you are comparing?

3. What are the two main features of the texts that you should try to compare and analyse?

EXAM PRACTICE

Spend about 5 minutes reading the extracts, then 20 minutes answering the question.

1. Look at Text C and Text D. In Text C, Sir Arthur Conan Doyle is writing to his sister about finishing his new novel. In Text D, Fay Weldon is remembering the time she showed her newly-published first novel to her neighbour, an established writer and university lecturer.

   Compare how the writers present their feelings about their own writing.   [16 marks]

Non-Fiction Exam Practice

Spend about 10–15 minutes reading the three texts, then complete one question from each section.

Text A

In this extract from her autobiography, Doris Lessing recalls a period during her childhood when she lived with two relatives, Bob and Joan, in Zimbabwe.

She liked me to run errands for her, walk to a near farm to fetch a recipe or take a present of vegetables. She liked me to feed the dogs, clean out their kennels, help with the cow. But best of all was when she told me to go down to the vegetable garden.

I took two large baskets, smelling of herbs, from the hooks in the pantry, and walked off from the front of the house by myself: the dogs always went with Bob. It was a sandy winding path between musasa trees, a mile or so. Half-way to the garden, a hundred yards off in the trees, were granite boulders where the python lived. Anywhere near those rocks, when with Bob, the dogs were called to heel, and he had his rifle ready on the slope of his arm. 'A python can move as fast as a horse,' said he. 'A dog, that's what they like best. A python got poor Wolf, two years ago.' I always walked slowly past that ominous pile, looking hard for the python. I saw it once, a grey coil, motionless in dappled light, easy to mistake for granite. My feet took me off in a spasm of terror as fast as I could go down to the garden, though I would have to return this way and now the python knew I was there he would… delicious terror, because I did not believe the python was interested in me. There were pythons on our farm and we often saw them, and I had never been chased by a snake speeding through the grasses. They were always sliding off as fast as they could go.

I stopped before reaching the garden, and stood sniffing that air soaked with herbs, tomatoes, the clean smell of peas. The garden was a half acre fenced to keep the duiker* out, but baboons sometimes got in and threw aubergines and green peppers around, and made holes where they dug up potatoes. The tomatoes sent out a smell so strong it made me giddy. A row of them, yards long, of plants as tall as a man, weighted with green tomatoes, yellow tomatoes, green tomatoes red-streaked which I sometimes had to pick for chutney – and so many ripe tomatoes there was no hope of ever picking even half of them. I filled the baskets with these dead ripe, heavy, aromatic, scarlet tomatoes, added bunches of thyme and parsley from beds crammed full of herbs, and went out, carefully fastening the gate…

I walked slowly back up the long path, feeling the heat get to me, and the tomatoes dragged my arms down. I did not run now as I passed the python's territory, though I watched the grasses for a rippling movement that meant he was coming for me. Slowly I went on, listening to the birds, the birds, the birds of Africa, and particularly the doves, the slow sleepy sound seducing you into daydreams and longing.

(from *Under My Skin*, by Doris Lessing)

*duiker = a small antelope

Text B

Five Children And An Allotment

Debbie Webber, who blogs at Carrots and Kids, explains how she runs a school gardening club and tends an allotment while looking after her five children.

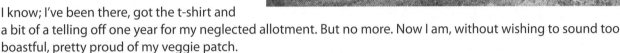

Let's face it, allotments are hard work. And family life? That can be just as hard, particularly if your children are young. Add the two together and you could be left wondering why you waited so long for your precious plot.

I know; I've been there, got the t-shirt and a bit of a telling off one year for my neglected allotment. But no more. Now I am, without wishing to sound too boastful, pretty proud of my veggie patch.

We've had our allotment in our South Downs village for seven years and during that time we've also increased our family from five to seven. Yes, we have five children. I've also added to the mix a school gardening club and, at home, a greenhouse and three raised veggie beds. I am getting used to the "how do you do it?" questions.

I've been wracking my brains and can't come up with a magic formula. I'm not sure how I do it. Actually, I don't think I do anything special, after all I don't work outside the house, but I am doing things differently this year.

Although the allotment is a family affair, it is primarily mine. My place to be on my own (pretty important for much-needed head clearing and peace). I escape here for at least two hours a week. My favourite time is very early in the morning, allowing me to get home before most of my family have opened their eyes.

I also have the luxury of two mornings free when my youngest are at nursery so, if I can, I nip up to the plot then. This doesn't happen as often as I like. Quite often the two-and four-year-old will accompany me on a quick weekday visit, playing with worms, a truck and in their digging hole while I weed. On these occasions I go without tools which prevents me from expecting to get on with other jobs and, therefore, stressed when I can't.

And that's the other key – expectations. Mine are horrendously low, both inside the house and out.

If I'm with the family at the plot on a weekend I really don't expect to get much done. It is also the one place where I refuse to get stressed. Peas been munched? Better sow some more. Not got all my to-do list done? There will be another chance. Dreams of keeping my family in veggies all year round? Lovely, but unlikely. I refuse to think of my allotment as work so I potter slowly, stopping often and drinking coffee always.

At home cobwebs don't register and the dishwasher always seems to need loading/unloading. But no one seems to get stressed about my lack of housekeeping skills (luckily) as gardening takes priority.

And that's the other point – gardening, and in particular growing vegetables, makes me gloriously happy. I get to do something I love which also benefits my family in lots of ways, not least of all having a happy, calm mother.

(from *The Guardian*, 19/06/09)

Text C

Heinz Tomato Ketchup

Paul Griffiths' mum had decided to abandon the usual birthday party of musical bumps and jelly in favour of tea and a trip to the cinema. We could have fish fingers and chips or sausage and chips. Some of the boys had both, but being a well-brought-up and somewhat timid nine-year-old, I felt that might be seen as greed. (It wasn't, it was just boys being boys, but that was a concept I had yet to master.)

The other boys were boisterously waving around a bottle of Heinz tomato ketchup, hitting it hard on the bottom, its open neck pointing alarmingly at the plate then swinging violently to less suitable targets. It was the first time I had eaten anything other than birthday cake in anyone else's home. It was also the first time I had encountered the joy of wielding a tomato ketchup bottle. Heinz, which is, I suppose, what one means when one mentions tomato ketchup, was banned in our house, and waving the bottle around like a loaded cannon looked enormous fun to a nine-year-old.

…the first experience of ketchup at Paul's party had a lot to live up to. To be honest, it was a bit of a let-down, being sweeter and rather less spicy than I had expected, but it was still red and thick and came in a bottle you had to thump. What's not to like? But despite there being something slightly tawdry* about a cold plate on its way to the washing up smeared with the remains of bacon, egg and tomato ketchup I have always wanted to like it more than I actually do.

Heinz tomato ketchup, surely the most famous commercial product after Coca-Cola, was launched in 1876, a ready-made version of the slow-cooked home-made 'catsup' of the American Deep South. Traditionally, catsup was made by boiling up tomatoes and seasoning them with cayenne, sugar and vinegar, cloves and cinnamon, and carried a certain amount of interest in its piquant* flavour and smooth, but not too smooth, texture. It had rough edges that made it sing in the mouth, and a clever balance of sweetness and acidity. Heinz seized the general idea, removed the rough edges and bottled it. They cleverly held on to the slow cooking bit by making sure the commercial sauce was thick enough to emerge only very, very slowly from its bottle.

There are many for whom the presence of the five-sided bottle is as essential to a meal as salt and pepper. Indeed, I once worked with a top chef who splattered it over everything he ate, though admittedly not until his boss and the customers had departed.

(from *Eating For England*, by Nigel Slater)

*tawdry = bright and showy but cheap and low quality
*piquant = a nicely sharp taste

Section 1
Exam Focus – Finding Information

Text A
1. Identify three chores that Doris has to do whilst living with Bob and Joan. [3 marks]
2. What do you learn about Doris's time spent living with Bob and Joan? [6 marks]

Text B
3. Identify three facts about Debbie Webber. [3 marks]
4. What do you learn about Debbie's attitude to gardening? [6 marks]

Text C
5. Identify three facts about tomato ketchup. [3 marks]
6. Identify three opinions about tomato ketchup. [3 marks]
7. Select three of the following statements that are true: [3 marks]
    a. The boys were going on a trip to the cinema.
    b. Nigel always had tomato ketchup at home.
    c. Nigel loved the taste of tomato ketchup.
    d. He thinks ketchup is quite fun.
    e. He thought the ketchup was too spicy.
    f. Ketchup is based on a sauce called catsup.

Section 2
Exam Focus – Language and Structure: Thoughts and Feelings

Text A
1. a. Select one phrase that shows Doris liked going to the vegetable garden. [1 mark]
   b. Explain how your phrase shows that Doris likes going to the vegetable garden. [1 mark]
2. How does the writer use language to show how much she loves the vegetable garden? [6 marks]
3. How does the writer use language and structure to show her childhood fear about the python? [12 marks]

Text B
4. a. Select one phrase that shows Debbie is pleased with her allotment. [1 mark]
   b. Explain how your phrase shows that Debbie is pleased with her allotment. [1 mark]
5. How does the writer use language to show the pros and cons of having an allotment? [6 marks]
6. How does the writer use structure to show the pros and cons of having an allotment? [6 marks]

Text C
7. a. Select one phrase that shows Nigel Slater thinks ketchup is fun. [1 mark]
   b. Explain how your phrase makes ketchup sound fun. [1 mark]
8. How does Slater use language to criticise tomato ketchup? [6 marks]
9. How does Slater use language and structure to make tomato ketchup sound good? [12 marks]

Section 3
Focus – Language and Structure: Engagement

Text A
How does the writer use language and structure to make her childhood memories interesting to the reader? [12 marks]

Text B
How does the writer use language and structure to engage the reader? [12 marks]

Text C
How does the writer use language and structure to make his thoughts about Heinz Tomato Ketchup entertaining to read? [12 marks]

Section 4
Exam Focus – Comparing Texts: Similarities and Differences

1. Look at Text A and Text B. What similarities and differences can you find in the two writers' lives? [6 marks]
2. Look at Text A and Text C. What similarities and differences can you find in the behaviour of the children? [6 marks]

Section 5
Exam Focus – Comparing Texts: How Ideas and Attitudes are Conveyed

1. Look at Text A and Text C. How do the two writers convey their enjoyment of food? [16 marks]
2. Look at Text A and Text B. How do the two writers convey their love of nature and being outdoors? [16 marks]

Ideas and Themes

You need to be able to show your basic comprehension of a text – finding information and supporting it with evidence.

Finding Information

You need to be able to find information about a specific theme that appears in a text, such as the weather, nature, emotions, or activities.

A question like this is not asking you to explain how ideas are conveyed; it is simply asking you to find related information.

> **Sample Question:** List four changes in the natural world in the text.
>
> It was nearing the end of autumn and the leaves were turning a golden brown. Some trees had already lost their leaves and now stood cold and grey, like huge witches' fingers pointing at the weak sun. The flowers of summer had all died and birds searched eagerly for food amongst the bushes. A hedgehog shuffled calmly along and prepared itself for hibernation. Winter was coming. As the children entered the garden, running and screaming, the birds squawked in panic and flew to the skies. As feet pounded against the ground, the hedgehog hid under some wilted leaves and curled into a spiky ball.
>
> You might write:
> - *The autumn leaves are changing colour.*
> - *Some trees have already lost all their leaves.*
> - *The flowers are dead.*
> - *The hedgehog is getting ready to hibernate over winter.*

Supporting Ideas With Quotations

In order to show that you have understood what you have read, you need to be able to support statements about a text with quotations.

Remember, if you are only asked to find quotations (not analyse them), just note them down and do not waste time writing about them.

For example, if you were asked to find two quotations from the previous extract to show that it isn't very warm, you might select:
- 'now stood cold and grey' or 'weak sun'
- 'prepared itself for hibernation' or 'Winter was coming'.

Identifying Changes

In a text, you need to be able to identify where and how things change. This could be a change in weather, attitude or behaviour.

You should be able to pick out a quotation and explain why it shows change.

> **Sample Question:** Explain how the behaviour of the wildlife changes when the children arrive.
>
> You might write:
> *At first the birds seem quite calm and happy, 'searched eagerly for food'. However, when the children arrive they are scared and try to get away from the garden, 'squawked in panic and flew to the skies'.*

Read this extract before attempting the Quick Test and Exam Practice questions.

Vera Claythorne, in a third-class carriage with five other travellers in it, leaned her head back and shut her eyes. How hot it was travelling by train today! It would be nice to get to the sea! Really a great piece of luck getting this job. When you wanted a holiday post it nearly always meant looking after a swarm of children—secretarial holiday posts were much more difficult to get. Even the agency hadn't held out much hope.

And then the letter had come.

'I have received your name from the Skilled Women's Agency together with their recommendation. I understand they know you personally. I shall be glad to pay you the salary you ask and shall expect you to take up your duties on August 8th. The train is the 12.40 from Paddington and you will be met at Oakbridge station. I enclose five £1 notes for expenses.

Yours truly,

Una Nancy Owen.'

And at the top was the stamped address, *Soldier Island, Sticklehaven, Devon…*

Soldier Island! Why, there had been nothing else in the papers lately! All sorts of hints and interesting rumours. Though probably they were mostly untrue. But the house had certainly been built by a millionaire and was said to be absolutely the last word in luxury.

Vera Claythorne, tired by a recent strenuous term at school, thought to herself, 'Being a games mistress in a third-class school isn't much of a catch…If only I could get a job at some *decent* school'.

And then, with a cold feeling round her heart, she thought: 'But I'm lucky to have even this. After all, people don't like a Coroner's Inquest*, even if the Coroner *did* acquit me of all blame!'

…Suddenly, in spite of the heat in the carriage she shivered and wished she wasn't going to the sea.

(from *And Then There Were None*, by Agatha Christie)

*Coroner's Inquest = an investigation when the cause of someone's death has to be discovered

SUMMARY

- You need to be able to find information and ideas in a text.

- You need to be able to prove things with quotations and explain how things change.

- Keep your answers simple and concise; unless the question uses the word 'how' you do not need to waste time analysing effects.

QUESTIONS

QUICK TEST

1. Look at the first paragraph of the extract:

   a. What is the name of the character in the extract?

   b. What is the weather like on the day she is travelling?

   c. What has she just achieved?

EXAM PRACTICE

Spend 5 minutes reading the extract and about 15 minutes answering the questions below.

1. List four things that we learn about Vera Claythorne.   [4 marks]

2. List four things that we learn about Vera's journey.   [4 marks]

3. Select two quotations that show 'Soldier Island' is a popular topic for discussion.   [2 marks]

4. Explain the way Vera's attitude to her teaching job changes.   [2 marks]

5. Explain the way Vera's feelings about going to Devon change.   [2 marks]

Language and Structure: Characters and Feelings

You need to be able to identify what a character is like and what they are feeling, and analyse how this is shown through choices of language and structure.

Working Out What a Character is Like

In order to analyse how a character is being conveyed, you should start by thinking about what the character is like.

Focus on:
● Appearance
● Behaviour
● Speech
● Feelings and attitudes

Sample Question: How is the character of Wanda presented in this extract?

Wanda sets off <u>awkwardly</u>. She is, after all, an <u>awkward</u> woman, who was formerly an <u>awkward</u> girl with <u>big</u> girlish teeth and <u>clumsy</u> shoulders. The pram's swaying body seems to steer her at first, instead of *her* steering *it*. Such a chunky rolling oblong, black and British with its wambling, bossy, outsized keel. 'Excuse me', she says, and 'Sorry'. Without meaning to, she <u>forces people</u> over to the edge of the sidewalks, <u>crowds them</u> at the street corners, <u>even rubs up against them</u> with the big soft tyres.

(from *Dressing Up For The Carnival,* by Carol Shields, from *Collected Stories*)

Appearance: <u>big and ungraceful</u>; new mum (pram she can't control)?

Behaviour: <u>clumsy</u>

Speech: embarrassed

Feelings and attitudes: apologetic

Exploring How Character is Shown

When you have got some ideas about a character, support each one with a quotation and analyse how features of language or structure show your idea.

Look out for specific words, techniques, and features of structure. For example:

Big and ungraceful: **repetition** of 'awkward'; adjectives for lack of grace ('big' and 'clumsy')

Clumsy: pattern of three verbs ('forces… crowds… rubs')

Embarrassed and apologetic: short phrases ('Excuse me… Sorry.')

Example
You might start:
Wanda is presented as physically large and ungraceful, 'an awkward woman, who was formerly an awkward girl'. The repetition of the adjective 'awkward' (also appearing, the sentence before, in the adverb 'awkwardly') suggests she looks uncoordinated. This physical image is emphasised through more adjectives when she is described as having 'big' teeth and 'clumsy' shoulders.

Wanda's behaviour is presented as clumsy…

Exploring Feelings and Attitudes

In a question like this, you do not explore everything about a character, only their specific feelings or attitudes.

Feelings means the emotions that someone is experiencing, such as happiness, fear, or sadness.

Attitudes means what someone thinks about another person or a subject, such as lack of respect, boredom or excitement.

Once you have identified the feeling or attitude in the extract, look for related key words as these will help you to find appropriate quotations to analyse. For example, if you thought the feeling in the text was happy you might look out for related nouns, adjectives, verbs, and adverbs, such as joy, delighted, smiling, and cheerfully.

Read this extract before attempting the Quick Test and Exam Practice questions.

Tamara has flung open her closet door; just to see her standing there is to feel a squeeze of the heart. She loves her clothes. She *knows* her clothes. Her favourite moment of the day is *this* moment, standing at the closet door, still a little dizzy from her long night of tumbled sleep, biting her lip, thinking hard, moving the busy hangers along the rod, about to make up her mind.

Yes! The yellow cotton skirt with the big patch pockets and the hand detail around the hem. How fortunate to own such a skirt. And the white blouse. What a blouse! Those sleeves, that neckline with its buttoned flap, the fullness in the yoke that reminds her of the Morris dances she and her boyfriend, Bruce, saw at the Exhibition last year.

Next she adds her new straw belt; perfect. A string of yellow beads. Earrings, of course. Her bone sandals. And bare legs, why not?

She never checks the weather before she dresses; her clothes *are* the weather, as powerful in their sunniness as the strong, muzzy early morning light pouring into the narrow street by the bus stop, warming the combed crown of her hair and fuelling her with imagination. She taps a sandaled foot lightly on the pavement, waiting for the number 4 bus, no longer just Tamara, clerk-receptionist for the Youth Employment Bureau, but a woman in a yellow skirt. A passionate woman dressed in yellow. A Passionate, Vibrant Woman About to Begin Her Day. Her Life.

(from *Dressing Up for the Carnival*, in *Collected Stories*, by Carol Shields)

SUMMARY

- If you are exploring character, look for appearance, behaviour, speech, and attitudes or feelings.

- If you are exploring just feelings or attitudes, focus on the character's emotions or what they think about a specific subject.

- Make sure you comment on the effect of specific words, techniques and sentence structures.

QUESTIONS

QUICK TEST

1. What different things should you look for when exploring what a character is like?

2. Why do you need quotations when analysing a character or their feelings and attitudes?

3. In the first line of the extract, what might the verb 'flung' suggest about Tamara's feelings?

EXAM PRACTICE

Spend 5 minutes reading the extract and about 15 minutes answering the questions below.

1. How does the writer use language and structure to present the character of Tamara?
   [8 marks]

2. How does the writer use language and structure to show Tamara's attitudes towards her clothes?
   [8 marks]

Language and Structure: Setting and Mood

You need to be able to analyse how a setting is being conveyed and how a writer creates a specific mood in their writing.

Setting

If you are analysing the setting in an extract from a fiction text, start by underlining all the phrases and sentences about the place you are focussing on.

Then think about what these lines tell you about the place (for example, is it inside or out, old or new, luxurious or squalid, etc.).

Mood

If you are asked about mood or atmosphere, you are expected to explore the general feeling or **tone** conveyed to the reader. This could be about a situation (such as a happy children's party) or a setting (like a creepy graveyard).

Improve your vocabulary so you can identify different moods, such as: sad, happy, exciting, calm, scary, tense, desperate, romantic, etc. Also learn synonyms for these moods to help you identify different aspects or intensity of a mood. For example:

Tense

uneasy > anxious > suspenseful > thrilling > climactic

Synonyms are particularly useful if you are asked to analyse how a mood is built up.

For example, if you were analysing how tension is built up, you would be exploring where characters feel increasing mental or emotional strain. You might start by analysing how a character is made to seem uneasy, before analysing how this turns into anxiety and suspense with the reader feeling on the edge of their seat. Then you might move on to analyse where the tension heightens to a thrilling level and finally climaxes.

Analysing Setting and Mood

You could be asked to analyse setting, mood, or how the two combine.

For each idea that you come up with, support it with a quotation and then analyse how features of language or structure are being used by the writer.

> **Sample Question:** How does the writer use the setting to create an unwelcoming mood?
>
> Within a quarter of an hour we came to Miss Havisham's house, which was of old brick, and dismal, and had a great many iron bars to it. Some of the windows had been walled up; of those that remained, all the lower were rustily barred. There was a courtyard in front, and that was barred; so we had to wait, after ringing the bell, until someone should come to open it.
>
> (from *Great Expectations*, by Charles Dickens)
>
> You might write:
> *The writer uses repetition to make the house seem unwelcoming, 'many iron bars… rustily barred… and that was barred'. This repeated detail presents the house as a prison that no one enters or leaves. The adjective 'iron' increases the idea that the bars keep everyone out, whilst the adverb 'rustily' suggests the house has been like this a long time.*
>
> *The writer also uses images of darkness to make the house seem unwelcoming…*

Read this extract before attempting the Exam Practice questions.

I crossed the staircase landing, and entered the room she indicated. From that room, too, the daylight was completely excluded, and it had an airless smell that was oppressive. A fire had been lately kindled in the damp old-fashioned grate*, and it was more disposed to go out than to burn up, and the reluctant smoke which hung in the room seemed colder than the clearer air,—like our own marsh mist. Certain wintry branches of candles on the high chimney-piece faintly lighted the chamber; or it would be more expressive to say, faintly troubled its darkness. It was spacious, and I dare say had once been handsome, but every discernible* thing in it was covered with dust and mould, and dropping to pieces. The most prominent object was a long table with a tablecloth spread on it, as if a feast had been in preparation when the house and the clocks all stopped together. An epergne* or centre-piece of some kind was in the middle of this cloth; it was so heavily overhung with cobwebs that its form was quite undistinguishable; and, as I looked along the yellow expanse out of which I remember its seeming to grow, like a black fungus, I saw speckle-legged spiders with blotchy bodies running home to it, and running out from it, as if some circumstances of the greatest public importance had just transpired in the spider community.

I heard the mice too, rattling behind the panels, as if the same occurrence were important to their interests. But the black beetles took no notice of the agitation, and groped about the hearth* in a ponderous elderly way, as if they were short-sighted and hard of hearing, and not on terms with one another.

(from *Great Expectations*, by Charles Dickens)

*grate/hearth = different words for a fireplace
*discernible = visible
*epergne = dining table ornament like a big bowl

SUMMARY

- Mood or atmosphere means the main emotion, feeling or tone in the extract.
- Use synonyms to explore different aspects of the mood.
- Think about how words, phrases, and sentence structures show what the mood or setting is like.

QUESTIONS

QUICK TEST

1. What does mood or atmosphere refer to?

2. Name four synonyms each for 'happy', 'calm', and 'scary'; put them in order of intensity.

3. What does 'tension' mean?

EXAM PRACTICE

Spend 5 minutes reading the extract and about 20 minutes answering the questions below.

1. How does Charles Dickens use language and structure to describe the room? [8 marks]

2. How does Charles Dickens use language and structure to create a sinister atmosphere?
   [12 marks]

Narrative Structure

You need to be able to explore how a text has been organised in order to develop ideas and engage the reader.

Structural Devices

You should be aware of the different ways in which a story can be told and the effects that these different devices can have. For example:

First person narrative	Emphasises thought and emotion. Can heighten suspense as the narrator doesn't know everything.
Third person narrative	Allows more breadth of character, setting, and events.
Linear narrative	Events happen in a familiar, **chronological** order, helping to establish plot.
Non-linear narrative	Events are not chronological (such as flashbacks) so we focus on an idea or theme, rather than plot.
Dual narrative	Two different narrators tell the story, allowing different viewpoints.
Multi-form	Other types of writing are included, such as diary entries, texts, or newspaper cuttings, to add variety and realism.
Shifts in mood	Changes in mood can grip the reader and keep us thinking.
Plot twist	Surprising the reader, rather than being obvious, creates a more enjoyable read.
Cliffhanger	Ending a paragraph or chapter with a problem makes us read on for the resolution.

Narrative Organisation

Always think about the extract in terms of start, middle, and end. What do the first few paragraphs do? How is this developed in the middle? What is revealed, changed or resolved in the last few paragraphs?

When exploring how a story is setting out to engage the reader, think about what it is doing:
- Is your extract establishing character, or setting, or plot? Or a combination of these things?
- Is your extract building up a particular mood, such as tension, excitement or mystery?

Once you know what it is doing, you can explore how this is achieved.

You will need to quote and comment on your quotations, but keep focussing on *how* the organisation of the text is engaging the reader (rather than the effects of specific words and images).

For example, an answer might start like this:

The extract engages the reader by gradually introducing the character of Mr Jackson.

At first, to get us thinking, the third person narrative only gives glimpses of the character, such as, 'a shadow passed through the hallway' or 'his fingertips drummed on the desk'. The author does not tell us much about the character, not even his name, which creates a sense of mystery. We only find out it's a man at the end of the second paragraph.

The middle of the extract begins to tell us more about his appearance, making us piece together our own image of him, but it holds back key information about his characteristics. For example, we find…

Read this extract before attempting the Exam Practice question.

At last there came a time when the driver went further afield than he had yet gone, and during his absence, the horses began to tremble worse than ever and to snort and scream with fright. I could not see any cause for it, for the howling of the wolves had ceased altogether. But just then the moon, sailing through the black clouds, appeared behind the jagged crest of a beetling, pine-clad rock, and by its light I saw around us a ring of wolves, with white teeth and lolling red tongues, with long, sinewy limbs and shaggy hair. They were a hundred times more terrible in the grim silence which held them than even when they howled. For myself, I felt a sort of paralysis of fear…

All at once the wolves began to howl as though the moonlight had had some peculiar effect on them. The horses jumped about and reared, and looked helplessly round with eyes that rolled in a way painful to see… I called to the coachman to come, for it seemed to me that our only chance was to try to break out through the ring and to aid his approach. I shouted and beat the side of the calèche*, hoping by the noise to scare the wolves from that side, so as to give him a chance of reaching the trap. How he came there, I know not, but I heard his voice raised in a tone of imperious command, and looking towards the sound, saw him stand in the roadway. As he swept his long arms, as though brushing aside some impalpable obstacle, the wolves fell back and back further still. Just then a heavy cloud passed across the face of the moon, so that we were again in darkness.

When I could see again the driver was climbing into the calèche, and the wolves had disappeared. This was all so strange and uncanny that a dreadful fear came upon me, and I was afraid to speak or move… We kept on ascending, with occasional periods of quick descent, but in the main always ascending. Suddenly, I became conscious of the fact that the driver was in the act of pulling up the horses in the courtyard of a vast ruined castle, from whose tall black windows came no ray of light, and whose broken battlements showed a jagged line against the moonlit sky.

(from *Dracula*, by Bram Stoker)

*calèche = a horse-drawn carriage

SUMMARY

- Think about how the start, middle, and end provide different things to engage the reader.
- Explore the effect of any specific structural devices.
- Consider how a mood is established and developed.

QUESTIONS

QUICK TEST

1. What different effects can a first person narrative offer compared to a third person narrative?

2. What is the effect of a cliffhanger?

3. What three sections can you divide an extract into?

EXAM PRACTICE

Spend 5 minutes reading the extract and about 10 minutes answering the question below.

1. This extract is from the final page of chapter 1 of Bram Stoker's novel, *Dracula*. The narrator, Jonathan Harker, is travelling in a horse-drawn carriage through the mountains of Transylvania.

   How does the writer structure the text to interest you as a reader?

   You could include:
   - The mood that the writer creates
   - What the writer focuses you on at the start of the extract
   - How and why the writer changes the focus as the extract develops
   - How the writer brings the chapter to an end.
   [8 marks]

Engaging the Reader

You need to be able to explore how a full range of features are used to engage the reader.

Language

Look out for powerful words, phrases, and techniques that have been used to describe character, setting, or events in interesting ways. Think about the kind of mood that the language creates in the extract.

Sentence Structure

Identify different punctuation and different sentence types or lengths that have been used to emphasise ideas, get the reader to think, or surprise the reader.

Narrative Structure

Make sure you read the question to find where in a story the extract is from, such as the opening page or the end of a chapter. This will affect how the writer has organised their ideas. Think about how the start, middle, and end of the extract introduce or develop ideas. Try to spot any narrative devices being used and think about their effect.

Sample Question: How does this extract, the opening of Fay Weldon's novel *Puffball*, try to engage the reader?

Many people dream of country cottages. Liffey dreamed for many years, and saw the dream come true one hot Sunday afternoon, in Somerset, in September. Bees droned, sky glazed, flowers glowed, and the name carved above the lintel, half-hidden by rich red roses, was Honeycomb Cottage and Liffey knew that she must have it. A trap closed round her.

(from *Puffball*, by Fay Weldon)

Possible ideas:
- Character of Liffey introduced. Fulfilled. Repetition of 'dream' followed by it coming true.
- Setting established. Perfect countryside: list form, different senses, **alliteration**, mood.
- Cliffhanger at the end of the paragraph. Short sentence. Links back to sibilance – a warning? 3rd person narrative makes this more effective.

You might write:

The opening introduces the main character: 'Liffey dreamed for many years, and saw the dream come true'. The repetition of 'dream' suggests she is an idealist or a romantic, and the end of the sentence makes her sound fulfilled and happy.

The setting is also established, 'one hot Sunday afternoon, in Somerset, in September. Bees droned, sky glazed, flowers glowed'. Different senses (sight, touch, and sound) are used to help the reader imagine a perfect countryside setting. Metaphor is also used ('flowers glowed') to make the place seem magical. The list form builds up these different images to create a mood of happiness and relaxation. As well as this, alliteration (first in 'glazed… glowed' and later in 'rich red roses') links the words together which increases the sense of harmony.

The author then intrigues the reader by using a cliffhanger at the end of the paragraph, 'A trap closed round her.' This sudden short sentence creates a contrasting mood of danger, with the verb 'closed' suggesting restriction instead of relaxation. It also makes us look back at the previous sentences where the sibilance in 'Sunday… Somerset… September', creating a snake-like hiss, could be a warning of what is to come. The third person narrative makes this cliffhanger more gripping because we know something the main character doesn't.

Can you see different features of language, sentence structure and narrative structure being analysed in terms of how they engage the reader?

Read this extract before attempting the Quick Test and Exam Practice questions.

We were the Mulvaneys, remember us?

You may have thought our family was larger, often I'd meet people who believed we Mulvaneys were a virtual clan, but in fact there were only six of us: my dad who was Michael John Mulvaney, Sr., my mom Corinne, my brothers Mike Jr. and Patrick and my sister Marianne, and me—Judd.

From summer 1955 to spring 1980 when my dad and mom were forced to sell the property there were Mulvaneys at High Point Farm, on the High Point Road seven miles north and east of the small city of Mt. Ephraim in upstate New York, in the Chautauqua Valley approximately seventy miles south of Lake Ontario.

High Point Farm was a well-known property in the Valley, in time to be designated a historical landmark, and "Mulvaney" was a well-known name.

For a long time you envied us, then you pitied us.

For a long time you admired us, then you thought *Good!—that's what they deserve.*

"Too direct, Judd!"—my mother would say, wringing her hands in discomfort. But I believe in uttering the truth, even if it hurts. Particularly if it hurts.

For all of my childhood as a Mulvaney I was the baby of the family. To be the baby of such a family is to know you're the last little caboose* of a long roaring train. They loved me so, when they paid any attention to me at all, I was like a creature dazed and blinded by intense, searing light that might suddenly switch off and leave me in darkness. I couldn't seem to figure out who I was, if I had an actual name or many names, all of them affectionate and many of them teasing, like "Dimple," "Pretty Boy" or, alternately, "Sourpuss," or "Ranger"—my favorite. I was "Baby" or "Babyface" much of the time while growing up. "Judd" was a name associated with a certain measure of sternness, sobriety, though in fact we Mulvaney children were rarely scolded and even more rarely punished; "Judson Andrew" which is my baptismal name was a name of such dignity and aspiration I never came to feel it could be mine, only something borrowed like a Hallowe'en mask.

(from *We Were the Mulvaneys*, by Joyce Carol Oates)

*caboose = a small carriage attached to the end of a train

SUMMARY

- Try to find features of language, sentence structure, and narrative structure.

- Are you told where in a novel the extract is from? Is this important?

- Think about how character, setting, mood and plot are introduced and/or developed.

QUESTIONS

QUICK TEST

1. What three aspects of the writer's craft should you explore?

2. Why can it help you to understand where in a novel the extract is from?

3. How does the opening sentence of the extract (left) use language and structure to engage the reader?

EXAM PRACTICE

Spend 5 minutes reading the extract and about 15 minutes answering the question below.

1. Read the extract from Joyce Carol Oates's novel, *We Were the Mulvaneys*. The novel is a family saga set between 1955 and 1980. The extract is the opening of the novel.

   How does Joyce Carol Oates try to engage the reader? [16 marks]

Debating and Comparing

You need to be able to compare, debate and evaluate extracts of fiction.

How Far Do You Agree?

In the exam you may be given a statement about an extract of fiction and then asked to what extent you agree with the statement. This is testing whether you can evaluate and structure a simple debate. You might get a statement like:

"The writer creates a sinister mood effectively. It's like you're inside the haunted house with the narrator."

Debating and Evaluating

It is much easier to begin by agreeing with the statement. Using any bullet point prompts given to you as part of the question, find evidence that the statement is true.

Keep coming up with clear ideas, state evidence to support each idea, and analyse how the writer's use of language and/or structure links to your idea and to the truth of the statement.

Use phrases that indicate evaluation of how well the writer has achieved a certain effect. For example:
- This is particularly successful because…
- The best phrase the writer uses to show this is…
- The writer makes good use of adjectives to…

In order to show that you are debating the statement, you should also try to make a comment that provides a counter-argument. Depending on the content of your text, you might write just one paragraph on this or it might take up half of your essay.

Introduce your counter-argument with a connective phrase like: however, on the other hand, despite this…

It is very important that you do not suggest a different way of writing the text. Instead, you should analyse – for example – where a character hasn't been presented effectively.

Comparing

If you are given two texts to evaluate and compare, you need to come up with clear ideas about the two texts that link to the statement you have been given.

For example, if the statement was "The writer presents the two main characters as utterly dislikeable", you might start by simply agreeing with the statement and coming up with similarities in the ways the characters are made to seem horrible, such as the way they speak or look.

However, you might then argue partly against the statement by saying that one character only does horrible things, whilst the other character does a few kind things.

Then you might argue fully against the statement by exploring how, in both texts, things happen that actually make us feel a bit sorry for the two characters.

Just as you normally would when analysing a text, each of your ideas needs to be supported by quotations and comments on the effects created by the writers' uses of language and structure.

Read these extracts before attempting the Exam Practice questions.

Text A

"You are part of my existence, part of myself. You have been in every line I have ever read since I first came here, the rough common boy whose poor heart you wounded even then. You have been in every prospect I have ever seen since,—on the river, on the sails of the ships, on the marshes, in the clouds, in the light, in the darkness, in the wind, in the woods, in the sea, in the streets. You have been the embodiment of every graceful fancy that my mind has ever become acquainted with. The stones of which the strongest London buildings are made are not more real, or more impossible to be displaced by your hands, than your presence and influence have been to me, there and everywhere, and will be. Estella, to the last hour of my life, you cannot choose but remain part of my character, part of the little good in me, part of the evil. But, in this separation, I associate you only with the good; and I will faithfully hold you to that always, for you must have done me far more good than harm, let me feel now what sharp distress I may. O God bless you, God forgive you!"

In what ecstasy of unhappiness I got these broken words out of myself, I don't know. The rhapsody welled up within me, like blood from an inward wound, and gushed out. I held her hand to my lips some lingering moments, and so I left her.

(from *Great Expectations*, by Charles Dickens)

Text B

They were driving back towards Northfield, and were only five minutes from Miriam's house, when she became hysterical. She began crying again, and screaming through her sobs that her life meant nothing when she was away from him, that she was going to turn up at his house and confront Irene, that she would kill herself if he didn't leave his wife and come to live with her. Bill pulled over to the side of the road and tried, hopelessly, to calm her down. He began promising things, promises he knew that he could never keep. The noise of her crying and shouting seemed to go on for hours, like radio static at top volume. All he could do was to repeat again and again that he loved her, he loved her, he loved her. They had both lost control of what they were saying.

(from *The Rotters' Club*, by Jonathan Coe)

SUMMARY

- Start off by agreeing with the statement.
- Remember to select quotations and analyse the effectiveness of language and structure.
- Make evaluative comments about the techniques used by the writer.

QUESTIONS

QUICK TEST

1. What is the phrase 'How far do you agree?' asking you to do?
2. What sort of phrases can you use to show you are evaluating?
3. If the question is about two texts, what must you remember to do?

EXAM PRACTICE

Spend 5 minutes reading the extract and about 30 minutes answering either questions 1 and 2 or answering question 3.

1. In Text A, a young man called Pip has been in love with a rich girl since his childhood. He has bettered himself to impress her but finds out that she is to marry someone else. Realising that she will not change her plans, he tells her one final time how much he loves her.
   A student, having read Text A, said: "The writer gets Pip's feelings across so realistically that you can imagine his heartbreak."
   To what extent do you agree?   [16 marks]

2. In Text B, the writer describes a married man called Bill and the woman he has been having an affair with, Miriam. During a day out together, he has broken off the affair.
   A student, having read Text B, said: "The writer makes you feel really sorry for Miriam."
   To what extent do you agree?   [16 marks]

3. "In Texts A and B, love is presented as a painful experience."
   How far do you agree with this statement?
                                              [24 marks]

Fiction Exam Practice

Spend 5 minutes reading the extract below. It is the opening of Joyce Carol Oates's novel, *The Falls*. The extract describes an unnamed man committing suicide by throwing himself into Niagara Falls.

Then spend 1 hour and 20 minutes answering the questions that follow.

At the time unknown, unnamed, the individual who was to throw himself into the Horseshoe Falls appeared to the gatekeeper of the Goat Island Suspension Bridge at approximately 6:15 A.M. He would be the first pedestrian of the day.

Could I tell, right away? Not exactly. But looking back, yes I should have known. Might've saved him if I had.

So early! The hour should have been dawn except that shifting walls of fog, mist, and spray rising in continuous billowing clouds out of the 180-foot Niagara Gorge obscured the sun. The season should have been early summer except, near The Falls, the air was agitated and damp, abrasive as fine steel filings in the lungs.

The gatekeeper surmised that the strangely hurrying distracted individual had come directly through Prospect Park from one of the old stately hotels on Prospect Street. The gatekeeper observed that the individual had a "young-old pinched face"—"wax-doll skin"—"sunken, kind of glaring eyes." His wire-rimmed glasses gave him an impatient schoolboy look. At six feet he was lanky, lean, "slightly round-shouldered like he'd been stooping over a desk all his life." He hurried purposefully yet blindly, as if somebody was calling his name. His clothes were conservative, sombre, nothing a typical Niagara Falls tourist would be wearing. A white cotton dress shirt open at the throat, unbuttoned dark coat and trousers with a jammed zipper "like the poor guy had gotten dressed real fast, in the dark." The man's shoes were dress shoes, black leather polished "like you'd wear to a wedding, or a funeral." His ankles shone waxy-white, sockless.

No socks! With fancy shoes like that. A giveaway.

The gatekeeper called out, "Hello!" but the man ignored him. Not just he was blind but deaf, too. Anyway not hearing. You could see his mind was fixed like a bomb set to go off: he had somewhere to get to, fast.

In a louder voice the gatekeeper called out, "Hey, mister: tickets are fifty cents," but again the man gave no sign of hearing. In the arrogance of desperation he seemed oblivious of the very tollbooth. He was nearly running now, not very gracefully, and swaying, as if the suspension bridge was tilting beneath him. The bridge was about five feet above the white-water rapids and its plank floor was wet, treacherous; the man gripped the railing to keep his balance and haul himself forward. His smooth-soled shoes skidded. He wasn't accustomed to physical exercise. His shiny round glasses slipped on his face and would have fallen if he hadn't shoved them against the bridge of his nose. His mouse-coloured hair, thinning at the waxen crown of his head, blew in wan, damp tendrils around his face.

By this time the gatekeeper had decided to leave his tollbooth to follow the agitated man. Calling, "Mister! Hey mister!"—"Mister, wait!" He'd had experience with suicides in the past. More times than he wished to remember. He was a thirty-year veteran of The Falls tourist trade. He was in his early sixties, couldn't keep up with the younger man. Pleading, "Mister! Don't! God damn I'm begging you: *don't!*"

He should have dialled his emergency number, back in the tollbooth. Now it was too late to turn back.

Once on Goat Island the younger man didn't pause by the railing to gaze across the river at the Canadian shore, nor did he pause to contemplate the raging, tumultuous scene, as any normal tourist would do. He didn't pause even to wipe his streaming face, or brush his straggly hair out of his eyes. *Under the spell of The Falls. Nobody mortal was going to stop him.*

(from *The Falls*, by Joyce Carol Oates)

Ideas and Themes

1. List four things about the man who commits suicide. [4 marks]

2. Select two quotations that show the events take place in the morning. [2 marks]

3. Explain the way the gatekeeper's thoughts about the man change. [2 marks]

Language and Structure: Characters and Feelings

1. How does the writer use language and structure to present the character of the man who commits suicide? [8 marks]

Language and Structure: Setting and Mood

1. How does the writer use language and structure to describe the Niagara Falls? [8 marks]

2. How does the writer use language and structure to build up a sense of tension? [12 marks]

Narrative Structure

1. How does the writer structure the opening of her novel to interest the reader? [8 marks]

Engaging the Reader

1. How does Joyce Carol Oates try to engage the reader? [16 marks]

Debating and Comparing

1. A student, having read the extract, said, "The writer describes the gatekeeper really well; you feel so sorry for him."

To what extent do you agree? [16 marks]

Planning Your Writing

In order to achieve a good mark for your writing, it is important that you get used to planning your ideas.

Purpose, Audience and Form (PAF)

Before you start any writing, read the task carefully and make sure you understand the purpose, audience and form that you have got to meet.

- **Purpose** means the function of the writing. For example, to describe, inform or persuade.
- **Audience** means who the writing is addressing. This could be a group of people, such as adults, pensioners or students at your school; it could also be individuals like an MP, your head teacher or a friend.

- **Form** means what type of writing your answer should take, such as a letter, a magazine article or a speech. Different forms are written in different ways, especially how they start and end, so you need to be aware of that when you are writing. If you are unsure, look at some of the example answers on the next few pages to remind you what different forms look like.

Planning

Depending on the writing task you are given, you have a particular structure to follow. However, you can **plan** your ideas in any way that you like. Students often find mind-maps, flow diagrams and lists particularly useful.

One you have worked out your PAF, give yourself a few minutes to note down as many ideas as you can. Then read them through and keep your best ideas. You could also make a note of any suitable techniques of language or structure that you could use within each idea.

Ordering Your Ideas

It is important that, when you write, your ideas have an appropriate order. This could be chronological (the order in which things happen) or **thematic** (ordering ideas in a way that links together and is logical). This will make your work cohesive so the reader can follow your ideas easily.

Just look at the ideas in your plan and quickly number them in a logical way. Each number could also remind you to start a new paragraph.

Developing

Either when you are planning or when you are actually writing, always think of ways that you can develop your ideas. So instead of moving on as soon as you have written an idea, think about whether you can use language to emphasise it or build upon it. This could be done by adding evidence for non-fiction writing, or by adding **imagery** for fiction writing.

Your development is where you get the chance to show off your different skills as a writer. This will help you to achieve the higher bands.

Checking

Make sure you build in time to your writing for checking. A few minutes at the end of the task will allow you to check:

- spelling, punctuation and grammar
- that you have conveyed your ideas effectively and developed them fully.

Sample Task

Imagine you have been asked to write an article for the school website about your experiences of starting at the school. It is aimed at reassuring new pupils about their first day.

Example Plan

- Finding the bigger-looking school daunting

  (adjectives, exaggeration, contrast with primary school) **②**

- Being scared when I woke up in the morning

  (verbs, metaphor, short sentence to show terror) **①**

- Seeing all the new people and feeling lost

  (simile, make being lost into a joke, use a list for all the different things) **③**

- Making friends/ realising it would be alright

  (more positive adjectives than the start, finish with short reassuring sentence) **⑤**

- Being late to a lesson and panicking but it being fine

  (contrasting adjectives, use ellipsis for cliffhanger) **④**

SUMMARY

- Start by identifying purpose, audience and form.
- Come up with your ideas and put them in a suitable order.
- Think of ways to develop your work.
- Build in time for checking.

QUESTIONS

QUICK TEST

1. What does PAF stand for?

2. What are the two main ways you can order your writing?

3. What things should you try to check once you have written your exam response?

EXAM PRACTICE

1. Spend 5 minutes making a plan for the following task:
   Imagine you have been asked to write an article for the school website in its regular 'Free Time' section. Tell other students about one of your hobbies or interests.

2. Spend 5 minutes making a plan for the following task:
   'Recycling is actually really easy and if we don't do it now we're doomed.'

   Write an article for a broadsheet newspaper in which you explain your point of view on this statement.

Spelling

Spelling is important in the writing sections of both the English Language and Literature exams.

Learn While You Relax

Learning spellings can actually come as a side-effect of enjoying yourself!

One of the best ways to learn spellings is to read more and actually pay attention to the words and how they are spelled. As a break from your revision, read a magazine or a book (it doesn't matter whether it is fiction or non-fiction).

You can also play different word games (in magazines, online, as an app, or board games) such as *Scrabble*, *Words With Friends*, or *Spelling Bee*. If you and your friends have trouble with spelling, do not feel embarrassed: have a bit of fun and support each other.

Try to remember little spelling rules that you have used in the past, such as:
- I before E except straight after C (but only when the sound is EE)
- FRI the END of your friend

Subject Specific Words

Avoid making mistakes with words that should be familiar to someone studying English, especially if the word is already printed for you in the exam paper!

Here are some key subject specific words that you should learn:

> **Pronoun**, noun, adjective, verb, adverb
>
> Simile, metaphor, personification, image
>
> Character, setting, atmosphere
>
> Convey, imply, suggest
>
> Novel, fiction, non-fiction, poem
>
> Author, poet, playwright, novelist, writer
>
> Paragraph, sentence, stanza, quotation

Make sure you have also learned how to spell the titles and authors of the literature texts you are revising.

Homophones

Students often make careless errors with words that sound the same but have different meanings and spellings. Learn the homophones in the table below and, if you know you find them difficult, make a bigger list for friends and family to test you on.

buy (to purchase)	by (a preposition meaning 'near' or 'on')	bye (abbreviation of 'goodbye')
cite (to quote)	sight (to see)	site (a place)
heel (part of your foot)	heal (to make better)	he'll (abbreviation of 'he will')
pause (to wait)	paws (the feet of an animal)	pours (to pour liquid)
seas (like oceans)	sees (to see)	seize (to take by force)
there (a place)	their (ownership)	they're (abbreviation of 'they are')
to (a preposition of direction)	too (suggesting excess)	two (a number)
ware (items to be sold)	wear (to put on)	where (place)

Word Endings

Some students struggle with spelling the endings of words if they are being pluralised (more than one) or if the **tense** is changing (past, present, future, etc.).

If you know this is an area that you need to improve on, pay attention to word endings when you are reading and think about:

- When verbs change tense, which just add –ed or –ing (e.g. walk = walked/walking) and which ones double their final consonant (e.g. plan = planned, planning)?
- Which verbs change completely when put in the **past tense**, such as run = ran (not runned)?
- Which nouns end in –s for their plural (e.g. book = books) and which end in –es (e.g. class = classes)?

Notice that nouns ending with a consonant followed by a –y always change from –y to –ies for their plural, such as army = armies.

Read this extract before attempting the Practice question.

It is best to revise in small chunks of about thirty to fourty minutes and then to take a brake. Give yourself breaks of ten to fifteen minites and, in that time, do something that is enjoyeble and relaxing. Watching television, phoning a friend, readding a magazine, even having a cup of tea with you're mum can calm you down while what you have learned sinks in. Avoid doing things that will be stressfull though, such as having an argument with your brother or playing a game on your console that you've been struling to compleat all week.

When you revise, make use of techneques that you no are usefull to you. Some people like too read there notes and copie them out; others like to reshape thier notes into visual aids like mind-maps and flow diagrams; or perhaps you prefer writing out cue cards for people to test you with. You need to revise in a way that you can actually learn so if your old method isn't working try a knew one.

In order to acheive successfull revision over a period of several weeks or even months, you also need to take care of yourself. As sugested above, balance work with play so that you don't succumb to stress. Work hard but also do things that you enjoy otherwise you will spend all your revision time just resentting your notes rather than learning from them. In addishun to this, think about sleep, diet, and exercise. They're is no magic food to enhance your memory but eating well and getting plenty of vitamins will help you stay healthy and focused. This is why you also need to sleep appropriatly: two much and you'll allways feel lazy; to little and you'll be exhausted and unable to properly revise. Regular exercise – whether that's going for a run, having a quick game of football with your freinds, dancing, or swiming – is also a great way to help you relax and keep healthy.

SUMMARY

- Learn subject specific words that you are likely to use in your English exams.
- Make sure your use of homophones is secure.
- Check your understanding of word endings.
- Try to learn helpful spelling rules.
- Make sure you can spell the names of the authors and set texts you've studied.
- Play games and practise!

QUESTIONS

QUICK TEST

1. Which spelling is correct?

   a. auther, author, awthor

   b. playwright, playright, playwrite

   c. similie, simile, simille

   d. atmosphear, atmosfear, atmosphere

   e. sentence, sentance, sentense

   f. caracter, charactar, character

   g. Shakespeare, Shakespear, Shakspeare

PRACTICE

1. Look at the text opposite. Circle and correct all the spelling mistakes. There are 30 errors to find.

Grammar and Punctuation

You need to be able to use a variety of punctuation accurately and should avoid careless errors in your grammar.

Sentence Structures

In order to produce varied and sophisticated writing, you should try to use a range of sentence structures. You cannot just do this on the day so you need to practise consciously using them.

- **Simple sentences**
  These are short sentences that contain a single verb, such as 'The planet is in danger.' They are good for emphasising an idea, whether you're highlighting a point in non-fiction writing or creating atmosphere in fictional writing.

- **Compound sentences**
  These are two simple sentences joined by a **conjunction**, for example, 'The moon was hidden by clouds and a cold fog crept through the streets'. They are good for establishing ideas, settings, and characters.

- **Lists**
  This is a series of items separated by commas, such as, 'Recycling is fun, easy, cost-effective, and environmentally friendly'. They are good for building up an idea.

- **Complex sentences**
  These are simple sentences with additional information that is separated by a comma. For example, 'The woman stepped back quickly from the window, certain she had seen someone watching the house'. This kind of sentence should dominate your writing as it allows you to add detail. One half is called a **main clause** (the part that makes sense on its own) and the other half is called a **subordinate clause** (the part that does not make sense on its own). The subordinate clause can be placed before, after, or in the middle of the main clause. You should practise using it in different positions to add extra variety.

- **Minor sentences**
  These are 'fragments' or grammatically incomplete sentences that are used deliberately to emphasise a word, phrase, or idea. Like simple sentences,

they shouldn't be used too often. For example, 'The following morning, I woke up with a terrible headache. Throbbing and stinging'. The second sentence is a minor sentence to emphasise pain.

Apostrophes

Students often struggle with the rules of apostrophes but they are quite simple.

- Abbreviation, for example: he is = he's; would not = wouldn't. The apostrophe shows where a letter has been missed out.
- Single ownership, for example: Sara's mug; James's car; the cat's dinner. An apostrophe plus an s goes after the owner.
- Group ownership, for example: the girls' shoes; the two cats' dinner. An apostrophe (without an s) goes after the owners.
- Never use apostrophes to show a plural. For example, writing something like 'I saw three cat's having their dinner' is incorrect.

Capital Letters

Students often make silly mistakes with capital letters. Remember that you always need them at the start of a sentence.

You should also use them at the start of proper nouns. These are the names of people, establishments, towns and countries, etc. For example, Mr Smith taught at Greenside School in London.

A Terrible Mistake

Some students tend to write 'of' instead of 'have' in phrases like could have, might have, should have.

This is because when we say them aloud and abbreviate them to could've, might've, should've, the 've' sounds like 'of'. However, this is wrong!

Read these sample sentences and paragraph before attempting the Practice questions.

Sentence A
Its black cloak billowing in the breeze, the figure began to follow Holly towards the house.

Sentence B
The advancing figure seemed to merge with the darkness of the night, moving as softly as a whisper.

Sample Paragraph
Holly kept running. She didnt know where she was anymore but she knew there was no time to stop and look around. As Hollys feet pounded the pavement she felt her heart thumping through her ribcage. Buildings, hedges signposts, and parked cars all passed in a blur of panic and adrenalin. she had to keep going in case they were still behind her. Suddenly, it's familiar red doorway shining in the moonlight she recognised darrens house. It was hard to believe she had run so far. Daring to glance behind her Holly saw an empty street. She was alone but was she safe? As she headed for the red door, a dark figure stepped out from the shadows.

SUMMARY

- Use a variety of correctly punctuated sentences.
- Try to learn where and why commas are used so you can check your own accuracy.
- Remember the rules for using apostrophes.
- Avoid careless mistakes with capital letters.

QUESTIONS

QUICK TEST

1. Correct the apostrophes or capital letters in the following sentences.

   a. Jacks first day, cleaning at everton Football club, was going well.

   b. Although she loved them, shirley disliked cleaning her dogs kennels.

   c. In bristols city centre, dave was walking to waterstones to buy JK Rowlings latest book.

PRACTICE

1. Rewrite the complex sentences A and B to show the subordinate clause in the two alternative positions. Do not forget that, when the subordinate clause is placed in the middle of the main clause, you need commas either side.

2. Correct the sample paragraph for punctuation and capital letters. There are 10 errors to find.

Writing to Describe

You need to be able to use all your different writing skills to create an effective **descriptive** piece.

Language

When you are writing to describe, you need to use a range of techniques to help the reader visualise what you are trying to convey.

On a basic level, make sure you select interesting and specific verbs, adjectives, and adverbs. A sentence like, 'The man in the red shirt was going down the street', is bland and vague. You can improve it simply by selecting words and building them up more carefully. For example, 'The young man in the crimson short-sleeved shirt was running desperately through the bustling street'.

Build up your ideas by using imagery: similes, metaphors, and **personification**. This will allow you to create more interesting pictures that help the reader to imagine what is happening.

Incorporate a variety of senses – sight, smell, sound, touch, taste – in order to give the reader a fuller experience of your fictional world.

Sentence Structure

Examiners will also be looking to see if you have tried to use sentence structures for effect.

In order to include plenty of detail in your descriptions, make sure you are using complex sentences. However, you should also try to vary the position of your subordinate clauses so your writing does not seem formulaic. (Look back at pages 36–37 if you are unsure about this.)

Try to use lists to build up features of character, setting, and atmosphere, or use short sentences to emphasise certain details.

Think about using contrasts, repetition for effect, or patterns of three to highlight important information.

Now and again, make use of exclamation marks to suggest a stronger tone or ellipses to create mystery or unease.

Narrative Structure

Remember to structure your whole descriptive piece carefully, just as a professional writer would.

Think about how to create an effective opening that grabs the reader's attention and an ending that either resolves a situation satisfactorily or gets the reader wanting more (such as a twist or a cliffhanger). This can be done by choosing really dramatic language and using sentence structures to make them stand out. You can also consider linking the language and themes of the opening and the closing so there is a sense of completion.

Consider other features of narrative structure that you could use to make your description interesting to read:

- First or third person
  Which will best help to convey the story you want to achieve?
- Dual narrative
  Do you want more than one narrator in order to present different sides of a story? Perhaps one in the first person and one in the third person?
- Linear or non-linear
  Do you want your description to run chronologically or do you want to move backwards and forwards, perhaps using flashbacks?
- Form
  Are you simply going to tell a story, or do you want it to be – fully or partially – in the form of a diary, letters, witness statements, newspaper articles, etc.?

Sample Task

Write the opening part of a story set on a winter's night.

You might begin:

Darkness, cold, and fear; night had fallen in Harpole. Crystalline frost crept across the pavements, dusting everything with its icy fingers. Moonlight reflected in the rime, fighting dimly against the all-encompassing darkness. Like a blanket of despair, night wrapped itself around every landmark with only a few metres visible at any one time. It was dangerous to be out so late. The black void of midnight seemed filled with thoughts of murder and madness.

His trainers pressing into the frost with a crackle, Tristan made his way home from football practice. His bag thumped against his back as he hurried on his way, trying to ignore the strange cries of foxes in the fields and the owls shrieking from the trees. Despite being tired from football, the darkness had heightened his other senses and increased his nervousness. Desperate to get home, he had cut through the strange little village rather than following the main roads. It was a decision he wouldn't live to regret.

You could practise your use of varied language and sentence structures by adding two more paragraphs to this story opening.

SUMMARY

- Use a variety of descriptive techniques to convey your ideas in an interesting way.

- Use different sentence structures in order to emphasise ideas and keep your writing varied.

- Make sure you have effective opening and closing sentences.

- Consider using narrative structure to make your description more engaging.

QUESTIONS

QUICK TEST

1. What are the five senses?

2. What are the three different positions in which a subordinate clause can be placed, in relation to the main clause?

3. What sentence structure can you use to emphasise an idea?

4. What sentence structure can you use to build up an idea?

EXAM PRACTICE

Spend 5 minutes planning your response to one of the questions below.

EXTRA PRACTICE *Spend 50 minutes turning your plan into a full exam response.*
[40 marks: 24 for content and organisation; 16 for technical accuracy]

1. Write about a time you, or someone you know, were caught doing something wrong.

2. Write the opening part of a story set on a hot summer's day.

3. Imagine you are writing your autobiography. Describe your first experience of being scared.

Writing From a Stimulus

You need to be able to create an engaging piece of descriptive writing that is inspired by an image.

Do/Don't

Using a stimulus is a form of writing to describe, so you should use all the methods of language, sentence structure and narrative structure that are explored on pages 38–39.

Use the ideas in the image to develop your writing.

You should not just describe the image you are given. The examiners are not testing your ability to spot things in a picture; they are testing your ability to come up with creative writing via a stimulus.

Getting Inspiration

When looking at the stimulus image, ask yourself different questions to get yourself thinking about your creative work.

Consider who, what, where, when, why, how?
For example:
- When and where is this?
- What time of day and year is this?
- What is the atmosphere (sad, happy, sinister, etc.)?
- What events may have happened here?
- How might people be involved with this?
- What is interesting, eye-catching, intriguing?
- Are there small details that I could make important?

Example

Look at image 1 (below). What ideas might you come up with?

creepy story — Night time

cobwebs — Internal descriptions — shadows

haunted — Abandoned house — disrepair — clues like blood stains

Isolated setting — External descriptions — cold weather

creates danger — darkness

Perhaps two children on a dare. They spend the night and uncover the house's murderous past.

Look at image 2 (below). What ideas might you come up with?

- Scene of attack – crime story.
- Woman knocked down stairs.
- Start with this point or begin with the attack?
- Where is this? Her apartment block.
- The attacker stands over her but will make it look like an accident.
- Describe her falling down the stairs. In flashback, add the events that led up to this point.

Sample Task

Look at the two images on page 40. Choose one to inspire the opening of a story.

Possible, engaging opening sentences:

- As the dark clouds passed across the pale moon, a wolf howled at the night with bloodthirsty intent.
- The house stared back like a skull.
- Nature had taken over; ivy, trees, and nettles enveloped the house, as if to hide its dark secrets.
- As if in slow motion, she fell through the air like a beautiful doll.
- Her body lay crumpled at the bottom of the stairs; he stood at the top, unfeeling, without regret.
- She gasped her final breath and then all was silent.

Which of these opening sentences do you think are the best?

What makes them interesting and engaging?

How could you improve the ones that you do not like?

SUMMARY

- **Do not describe the image. Instead, use it to inspire and develop your creative writing.**

- **To get inspiration, ask yourself questions about the image and start shaping the answers into a story.**

- **Remember to use different features of language, sentence structure and narrative structure in order to create sophisticated and effective descriptive writing.**

QUESTIONS

QUICK TEST

1. Are you supposed to describe the image or use it to inspire you?

2. What kind of questions can you ask about the image to get yourself thinking?

3. What three areas of descriptive writing is it still important to use?

EXAM PRACTICE

Spend 5 minutes planning your response to one of the questions below.

EXTRA PRACTICE *Spend 50 minutes turning your plan into a full exam response.*
[40 marks: 24 for content and organisation; 16 for technical accuracy]

1. You are entering a creative writing competition. Write a description suggested by image 1.

2. Write the opening part of a sinister story, inspired by image 1.

3. Use image 2 to write the opening of a story.

4. Look at images 1 and 2. Write about an imagined frightening experience. You may wish to base your response on one of the images.

Writing to Inform and Explain

You need to be able to convey information and explanations clearly and in an engaging way.

Inform/Explain

Writing to inform means presenting the reader with information about a specific topic. You find this type of writing in newspaper reports about events or in class presentations about activities or experiences.

Writing to explain is similar but it also contains more detail about the reasons behind things, what we call cause and effect. You might find this type of writing in magazine articles about particular issues, job application letters (explaining why you are suitable for employment), or blogs that are giving their point of view about a certain topic.

Read the question carefully so you know exactly what the examiner wants from your response.

Organisation

If you are writing about a specific event that has happened, you will need to use a chronological structure. This will help the reader to clearly understand the order in which things happened. Use connectives of time and place to help you join your ideas.

However, if you are writing about a given topic, you should use a thematic approach. Write about a different aspect of your topic in each paragraph but try to make these aspects follow on from each other in a cohesive way. Use connectives of progression (e.g. in addition, furthermore, also) and connectives of cause and effect (e.g. as a result, because of this, consequently).

Key Features

Although these two types of writing contain opinion (such as an eye-witness's response to an event, or giving your views about a local issue), they should also contain a lot of facts.

If you are writing about a topic that you are not specifically involved in (such as a news report, or an article about recycling), you should write in the third person. This helps to keep your writing fact-based and impersonal.

If you are involved in the subject (for example, giving your point of view, applying for a job, or making a speech about an activity that you took part in), you should use the first person. However, remember that you still need to include lots of facts.

Make sure you include lots of detail. Try to imagine that the reader is coming to your writing to find things out. Consider the 5 Ws: who, what, when, where, why?

Keep concise. Including plenty of detail does not mean waffling so make sure that you are always relevant and to the point.

Sample Task

Write an article for a Sunday magazine's regular feature, 'Famous Person Party Invite', about the two well-known people you would invite to a party at your home. The people could be celebrities, sportspeople, inventors, etc. from the present or the past.

You might begin:

Without a doubt, Louis Smith would be my first choice as a party guest. As well as being an Olympic medal winner and a winner of Strictly Come Dancing, he has an interesting background.

Louis first became famous in 2012, after winning the silver medal for the pommel horse at the London Olympics. He had won bronze at the previous Olympics in Beijing and has taken part in many more competitions. I think the combination of hard work and success would make him a fascinating person to talk to.

I would like to ask him about his training regime: what it entails, how it affects his life, and whether there are days when it's so tough he just feels like giving up. It would also be interesting to know his feelings about how the Olympics changed his life and what it felt like to stand on a podium, receiving a medal, and knowing you are one of the world's top gymnasts.

One of the most interesting things about Louis, though, is his background. His mum was a struggling but loving single-parent and he suffered from ADHD at school. It would be moving and inspirational to listen to his stories about his childhood. Having coped with his difficulties, Louis fronted a documentary about ADHD; it would be intriguing to hear his opinions on society's attitudes towards the issue and the current ways it is treated.

My second choice for a party guest would be…

You could add your own section to this response, remembering to include lots of facts and to give a clear explanation of why you would invite your selected person to a party.

SUMMARY

- **Read the question carefully so you know exactly what you are informing about or explaining.**
- **Use the first person if the writing needs to be personal but third person if you are not directly involved.**
- **Include lots of facts.**
- **Be detailed but also concise.**

QUESTIONS

QUICK TEST

1. What type of connective is useful for linking paragraphs in an article informing about an event?

2. What types of connectives are useful in writing to explain?

3. Why are facts important in writing to inform and explain?

EXAM PRACTICE

Spend 5 minutes planning your response to one of the questions below.

EXTRA PRACTICE *Spend 50 minutes turning your plan into a full exam response.*
[40 marks: 24 for content and organisation; 16 for technical accuracy]

1. 'School uniform creates a barrier to learning.' Write an article for a broadsheet newspaper in which you explain your point of view about this statement.

2. Imagine your school has organised an exchange programme with a French school. You have been asked to write the text for a leaflet about your school, so the foreign students know what to expect when they arrive.

3. Write an article for the school website about someone you respect. This might be a friend, a relative, or a public figure.

Writing to Argue and Persuade

You need to be able to use different devices of language and structure to convey a viewpoint effectively.

What is the Difference?

When you write to persuade, you are trying to get your reader to think or do something.

If you are arguing, you are presenting your opinion about an issue and proving that you are right. You can be asked to do two different types of argument: one is simply arguing for or against a given issue; the other expects more balance, presenting your opinion followed by alternative views that include your counter-argument.

Build it Up!

Structure your writing carefully so that your viewpoint builds up in a cohesive, convincing way. The reader should be able to follow the thread of your thinking as this will get them on your side.

Make use of a range of connectives to emphasise that you are building up your viewpoint. When persuading, use connectives of sequence and progression. Here are some examples:

Sequence	Progression
Firstly	Moreover
Next	Similarly
Finally	As well as this

When you are arguing, you might also make use of connectives of contrast and of cause and effect. These might include:

Contrast	Cause and Effect
In contrast	As a result
On the other hand	Consequently
However	Therefore
While	Because of this

Rhetorical Techniques

Rhetorical techniques are used to convince readers or emphasise meaning. One way to learn them is by using the FORESTRY mnemonic:

- **F**acts
  Support your views with lots of facts; people are more convinced if they are given evidence.
- **O**pinions
  Convey your ideas powerfully; state your opinions as if they are true, avoiding weak phrases like 'maybe' or 'perhaps'.
- **R**hetorical questions
  Use these guided questions to get your reader thinking that you are right.
- **E**motion and **empathy**
  Use **emotive language** to make your readers feel something, such as respect, sympathy, or guilt; try to connect with their feelings as it is easier to win people round if they think you understand them.
- **S**tatistics
  Like facts, these will make your viewpoint sound researched; the examiner knows you can't actually research so make up some (realistic-sounding) figures.
- **T**riplets
  Organise parts of an idea into a pattern of three to emphasise a point.
- **R**epetition
  Deliberately writing a key word or phrase more than once can highlight an idea.
- **Y**ou
  Address the audience directly in order to make your viewpoint more convincing.

Sample Task

Write the text for a presentation that encourages your classmates to watch your favourite television programme or film.

You might begin:

Doctor Who is the world's longest running science-fiction programme. It is, quite simply, the best show on television.

Have you ever wondered what it would be like to travel through time and space, stepping on to alien planets or becoming part of historical events? Doctor Who allows you to do this on a Saturday night. The show is full of big ideas, monsters, robots, explosions, and lots of running. It manages to be funny, moving, exciting and intelligent. Every episode is gripping.

But Doctor Who is more than just a blockbuster on the small screen: it also shows you how to be a good person. The show is all about compassion and equality. The Doctor makes people better; he is the champion of the weak and vulnerable, and he never wields a gun. Aren't they qualities that we should all aspire to?

For over 50 years, the programme has enthralled generation after generation of viewers. The Doctor has faced Daleks, Sontarans, and Cybermen. He has saved lives, saved planets, and saved the whole universe.

Have you been watching? You should be.

Can you spot different rhetorical techniques being used in the paragraphs above?

SUMMARY

- If you are asked to argue, read the question carefully so you are clear about whether you are writing a balanced argument or one that is specifically for or against an idea.

- Organise your ideas and use connectives in order to build up your viewpoint effectively.

- Learn and use the FORESTRY mnemonic.

QUESTIONS

QUICK TEST

1. What is the purpose of writing to persuade?

2. What rhetorical techniques should the FORESTRY mnemonic help you to remember?

3. What different types of connectives might you use in writing to argue?

EXAM PRACTICE

Spend 5 minutes planning your response to one of the questions below.

EXTRA PRACTICE *Spend 50 minutes turning your plan into a full exam response.*
[40 marks: 24 for content and organisation; 16 for technical accuracy]

1. Write an article for your local newspaper in which you present the argument for and against the proposal to change the speed limit for all roads across the country to 40 mph.

2. Write a speech for your school assembly arguing either for or against the banning of mobile phones in school.

3. Write an article for the travel section of a local newspaper, persuading people to visit your favourite holiday destination.

Writing to Advise and Instruct

You need to be able to use your writing skills effectively in order to tell people what to do.

Give Instructions, Offer Advice

When you instruct, you simply tell people what to do (for example, a manual or a safety leaflet).

When you advise, you show empathy with a person's situation and suggest what they should do (for example, an 'agony aunt' letter or a blog on coping with stress). It is very important that writing to advise is confident but also has a friendly and supportive tone of voice. One way to achieve this is to offer alternatives; the reader may feel more encouraged if they can choose to follow the orders that they are most comfortable with.

Order and Structure

Both types of writing require a lot of **orders** (or **imperatives**) so people know what they should do. To keep these friendly in writing to advise, you should attach an empathising phrase before the order, such as 'Although talking to new people can feel awkward, you must make an effort to speak to people at your new school'.

To keep your orders clear, you need to put them in a logical order and join them together using connectives of sequence. In writing to instruct, these connectives should be quite simple (first, secondly, next, finally) but in writing to advise they should be more varied so they seem friendlier (to begin with, after this, once you have achieved that).

Modal Verbs

Modal verbs are used to show necessity, possibility, and ability. These will help you to emphasise your orders or advice. Learn the four modal verbs in the following table. Read the examples of modal verb being used and think about how they can help you to advise or instruct.

Modal verb	Advising…	Instructing…
Must	You must prove to your friends that they can trust you again.	You must turn off the electricity at the mains before continuing.
Need	You need to build up your confidence.	You need to attach the base first.
Should	You should try to ignore their nastiness and focus on your friends.	You should now attach the legs of the chair one by one.
Could	You could speak to a teacher about how you're feeling.	You could use scissors or a knife to cut the plastic.

Show You are Right

To encourage the reader to follow your advice or instructions, you need to use a few techniques to show that you are right.

First, address the reader using 'you', as this will make them feel the writing is personalised to their situation.

When instructing, add connectives of cause and effect. If you make it clear why something needs to be done, the reader will be reassured that you are an expert.

When advising, use some of the FORESTRY techniques of persuasion such as opinions, **rhetorical questions**, empathy, **triplets**, and repetition. This will help to convince your reader that your advice is worth following.

Sample Task

Write a speech to be given to your peers that offers advice about living a healthier lifestyle.

You might begin:
Good morning, I am here today to talk to you about how to get started on a healthier lifestyle.

I know that it's much easier just to sit on the sofa, watch television, and eat crisps, but everyone needs to exercise. Whether it's jogging, dancing, or hitting the gym, you should find the type of physical exertion that you enjoy so you can look after your body for tomorrow.

Coming up with a goal and setting yourself a routine is an excellent way to get yourself into the rhythm of regular exercise. Too often, we set ourselves unrealistic goals and this can be an obstacle to our success. You should start with a simple goal, like running for ten minutes every other night, or managing to swim 100 metres. Then you can aim for something more difficult once this has been achieved.

People often say they feel embarrassed going to the gym or going for a run. You worry that you look silly struggling with the weights or getting sweaty half way around the track but this is only in your head. Everybody else looks the same. So rather than focussing on what others might think, focus on what you want to achieve. Doesn't everyone want to feel fit and healthy?

To help you stick to your healthier lifestyle, you could try to get your friends involved…

You could add your own section to this response, remembering to make your advice friendly and supportive by combining orders with empathy and alternatives.

SUMMARY

- **Tell the reader what to do but, if writing to advise, include lots of empathy and alternatives so you seem friendly and supportive.**

- **Use modal verbs to emphasise your instructions or advice.**

- **Use different techniques to show the reader that you are right.**

QUESTIONS

QUICK TEST

1. How is the tone different in writing to instruct and writing to advise?

2. What are modal verbs?

3. What type of connectives should you use to make your ideas clear?

EXAM PRACTICE

Spend 5 minutes planning your response to one of the questions below.

EXTRA PRACTICE *Spend 50 minutes turning your plan into a full exam response.*
[40 marks: 24 for content and organisation; 16 for technical accuracy]

1. Write an article for the school website about how to deal with peer pressure.

2. Write the text for a leaflet, advising young people about staying safe on the Internet.

3. Write the text for a website, instructing people about staying safe on Bonfire Night.

Poetic Techniques

You need to be able to identify and analyse the effect of a range of poetic techniques in the exam.

Transferable Skills

A lot of 'poetic techniques' also appear in prose (both fiction and non-fiction) and drama. They are just ways of describing things. Use your wider knowledge of literature and creative writing as a foundation for this section.

Imagery

Poets use a range of techniques to build up pictures for the reader. These pictures contain the meaning of the poem and show us what the speaker is thinking or feeling.

Images

Any time a poet has used nouns, adjectives, verbs or adverbs to create a picture in the reader's head, they are creating an image. Identify the images being created by a poet and discuss their effect.

Recurring Imagery

Consider whether any of the images in the poem have a similar theme, such as nature, darkness, romance. This is called a recurring image and is used to make it clear what the poet is asking us to think about.

Simile

These are comparisons using 'like' or 'as'. Poets use similes to link a complex or unusual idea to something that we are familiar with. They help us to understand what the poet is trying to convey.

> **Example**
> The pain of his loss felt like a deep hole inside her stomach.

Metaphor

These are also comparisons but, whereas a simile uses 'like' or 'as', metaphors are written as if they are true. Often poets use them to make an idea more interesting or to make us see a familiar thing in an unusual way.

> **Example**
> A deep hole opened inside her stomach.

Extended Metaphor

Sometimes a metaphor can run through an entire poem, for example, if a poet was using the times of day as a metaphor for the stages of a love affair. When a poet does this, and it is the same comparison being used to explore different ideas, it is called an **extended metaphor**.

Personification

This is a type of metaphor but it is specifically when an object (a noun) or an idea (an abstract noun, such as hatred) is written about as if it has human qualities. This could be giving it physical attributes (like referring to the branches and twigs of a tree as arms and fingers) or it could be giving it emotional or behavioural attributes (such as saying that a building stared back at you).

Sounds

Poets often use different sounds in order to make important words, phrases, or images stand out. Do not think of them as conveying meaning, more emphasising it.

- Rhyme = when two words (usually at the end of lines) sound the same.
- Internal rhyme = when two words are rhymed within the poem for effect.
- **Alliteration** = when a series of words are given the same opening sound.
- **Sibilance** = when a series of words start with, or contain, 's' sounds (s, sh, z).
- **Plosives** = particularly hard sounds, at the start or within words (c, k, t, p, b, d).
- **Onomatopoeia** = words that actually sound like the sound they describe.

Read these examples of poetic techniques being used before attempting the Quick Test and Practice questions.

a. The constant banging from next door;
the crashing and beating.
It will not stop.

b. At the sight of her,
my long dead mother,
my mind unwraps and the memories flood out.

c. The old house watches me,
her walls and windows beckon me:
she wants me to enter; wants me.

d. It slid through the grass
then slithered towards my feet.
Danger! A snake.

e. When I touched his hand
it was as cold as ice
and I knew:
he'd never love me.

SUMMARY

- Remember that 'poetic techniques' also appear in other forms of writing so analyse them wherever you see them.

- Imagery is used to convey the poet's ideas in an interesting way that creates a picture in the reader's head.

- Different sounds are used to emphasise key words, phrases and images.

QUESTIONS

QUICK TEST

Look at the five different examples of poetic techniques.

1. Which one contains a simile?

2. Which one contains a metaphor?

3. Which one contains sibilance?

4. Which one contains plosives and onomatopoeia?

5. Which one contains personification?

PRACTICE

Check your answers to the five questions above and then try analysing the effects of the techniques.

1. How is the simile used to show what the man is like?

2. How is the metaphor used to show the poet's experience of seeing a photograph of his dead mother?

3. How is the sibilance used to emphasise different things?

4. How are the plosives and onomatopoeia being used to emphasise the poet's thoughts?

5. How does the personification convey the poet's relationship with where he used to live?

Structural Techniques

As well as commenting on language, you need to be able to explore the effects of different structural decisions made by the poet.

Reading a Poem's Structure

In order to explore how a poem works, it is important that you read it correctly. Because of the way in which poems are divided into lines, some students stop at the end of each line. You must not. Always read it sentence by sentence (from the capital letter to the full stop, even if that includes five or six *lines*).

If you do this, you can start to explore the types of sentences being used and what happens within the sentences.

What Does Structure Do?

The sentence structures in a poem are used to emphasise the ideas that the poet has introduced through language. Because of this, you should not just spot structural techniques. Only write about them if you can see them emphasising the meaning of the poem in some way.

Pauses and Enjambment

The poet's use of punctuation and their decisions about when to start new lines will create **pauses** when you read. Do not write about every pause that you see! However, you should think about whether any of the pauses are used for specific effect: to emphasise an idea or image.

If a poet does not put a punctuation mark at the end of a line and simply continues the sentence, it is called enjambment. It is particularly worth considering the effects of this if it happens at the end of a stanza:
- What is the effect of the pause that is created?
- Does it emphasise an idea at the end of the stanza or an idea at the start of the next, or does it divide two images in an interesting way?

Sentence Length

Always consider whether the length of the sentences is relevant to the meaning of the poem.

Poets regularly use short sentences to make an important idea stand out.

However, a very long sentence can also be important; sometimes, poets write a whole poem using only one sentence. Long sentences can be used to suggest that the speaker is involved in something that is continuous, or they haven't had time to stop, or perhaps they are really focussed on one event or feeling.

Sentence Types and Punctuation

The punctuation in a poem can show you if a poet is asking lots of questions (interrogatives) or including lots of **exclamations**. This can help you to understand what the speaker is thinking or feeling.

Also think about the function of the sentences. As well as asking questions or exclaiming, a sentence can state an idea or give an imperative (an order). This may be important to understanding the poem's meaning.

The poet might also use commas to create short or long lists. This can be done to build up a single idea in order to emphasise it.

Repetition

Poets often repeat meaningful words or phrases in order to highlight their importance to the reader.

Sometimes this is done in a more structured way, for example at the start of every other line or at the end of every stanza. When the repetition appears in a set place in this way, it is called **anaphora**.

Read these examples of structural techniques being used before attempting the Quick Test and Practice questions.

a. In your pale eyes,
    Those deep, deep eyes,
    I see your love

    Or your hate,
    Your deep, deep hate,
    Staring back at me.

b. How long will you be,
    will you think of me?
    Will your heart reach across that sea,
    thousands of miles,
    to feel close to me?

c. She cleans, she scrubs,
    she vacuums, dusts, and rubs;
    my mother's work seems never done.

d. Go! Take your selfish heart!
    Leave me alone, with mine torn apart.

QUESTIONS

QUICK TEST

Look at the four different examples of structural techniques.

1. Which one contains a list?

2. Which one uses short sentences and imperatives?

3. Which one features repetition and enjambment?

4. Which one uses interrogatives?

PRACTICE

Check your answers to the four questions above and then try analysing the effects of the structural techniques.

1. How is the list used to emphasise the meaning of the poem?

2. How are the short sentences and imperatives used to mirror the speaker's feelings?

3. What is the effect of the repetition of 'deep' in the first example?

4. What does the enjambment emphasise about the speaker's thoughts?

5. How are the interrogatives used to show the speaker's feelings?

Form

As well as commenting on specific words, images and sentence structures, you need to think about how the shape of the poem contributes to its meaning.

Stanzas

There are different names for stanzas, according to the number of lines they have, such as tercet (three lines), quatrain (four lines) or sestet (six lines).

Shape and Rhythm

Look at the 'shape' of a poem and consider whether it reflects the meaning of the poem. Each poem is different but here are some ideas to get you thinking.

If the poet is writing about something calm or restrictive, they might make the shape of their poem uniform (such as four quatrains). However, if the poet is exploring freedom or chaos, they could make the poem look more random (such as a tercet, then a sestet, and then a single line).

The same is true of the metre of the poem: this is the number of syllables that each line has and the pattern of stressed/unstressed beats that is created. If all the lines are of a similar length with a similar pattern of stressed/unstressed beats, the poet might be suggesting control; if they are all different lengths without a clear pattern of beats, the poet could be presenting confusion.

You should also consider rhyme scheme. If there is a clear rhyme scheme, such as rhyming couplets (which you can describe as *aabb*) or every other line rhyming (*abab*), the poet might be using this, again, to create uniformity.

However, the poem could be in blank verse (where lines are a similar number of syllables but do not rhyme) or even free verse (no rhyme or syllable pattern), which might show the poet presenting different degrees of freedom.

Keep an open mind and interpret the shape of the poem in relation to the poem's meaning.

Limericks

Limericks can be useful for securing your understanding of shape and metre.

> **Example**
> There was an old man with a beard,
> Who said, 'It is just as I feared!
> Two owls and a hen,
> Four larks and a wren,
> Have all built their nests in my beard!'
>
> From *Book of Nonsense,* by Edward Lear

Because they need to be memorable for children to recite, limericks have a highly shaped form.

The first, second, and fifth line always contain eight syllables.

These lines also have the same metre. Say the poem aloud and notice how the stress pattern is the same:

There	**was**	**an**	**old**
Unstressed	stressed	unstressed	unstressed

man	**with**	**a**	**beard**
stressed	unstressed	unstressed	stressed

The third and fourth lines are also the same. They contain five syllables and the same metre (unstressed, stressed, unstressed, unstressed, stressed).

The rhyme scheme for a limerick is always *aabba*, meaning the first, second and fifth lines rhyme, and the third and fourth lines rhyme.

Sonnets

There are lots of different poetic forms (such as ballads, odes and lyrical poetry). However, the form you are most likely to encounter is the sonnet, partly because Shakespeare wrote lots of them!

The sonnet is traditionally used in love poetry. It has 14 lines, a clear rhyme scheme and a regular metre called iambic pentameter (10 syllables per line, with five pairs of syllables in each line, each pair consisting of an unstressed and stressed syllable).

This form could look controlling or restrictive but, actually, it is used to intensify the poet's emotions. The writer pours their heart out in this small, box-like poem, and that heightens the passion.

Sonnets also include little features to emphasise ideas. For example, Shakespeare's sonnets end with a rhyming couplet that acts as a twist to either hammer home his point or get you to reconsider what he has previously said.

Dramatic Monologue

This is another form of poetry to look out for. Unlike the sonnet, it can be any shape that the poet likes. In a dramatic monologue, the poet takes on the role of a character who appears to be having a conversation with someone (but we never actually meet the audience or get their opinion).

Modern poets use this regularly. It is important to remember that poets are not always giving you their personal feelings. Often, they are imagining an experience. This is why it can often be better to say 'the speaker feels' rather than 'the poet feels'.

Read the following poem before attempting the Practice questions.

My Love is as a Fever…   **by William Shakespeare**

My love is as a fever, longing still
For that which longer nurseth the disease,
Feeding on that which doth preserve the ill,
The uncertain sickly appetite to please.
My reason, the physician to my love,
Angry that his prescriptions are not kept,
Hath left me, and I desperate now approve
Desire is death, which physic did except.
Past cure I am, now reason is past care,
And frantic-mad with evermore unrest;
My thoughts and my discourse as madmen's are,
At random from the truth vainly expressed;
    For I have sworn thee fair and thought thee bright,
    Who art as black as hell, as dark as night.

SUMMARY

- **All poems are different. You cannot learn what a form is representing; you have to interpret it once you have read and understood the poem.**

- **Look at the poem's 'shape' and consider whether it reflects the poem's meaning or ideas in any way.**

- **Try to use technical terms about form (such as stanza, couplet and dramatic monologue).**

QUESTIONS

QUICK TEST

1. What is the technical term for the number of beats and syllables in a line?

2. What is usually the subject matter of a sonnet?

3. What is a dramatic monologue?

PRACTICE

1. In the poem opposite, Shakespeare describes being in love as if it is an illness. He is head over heels in love with someone but in pain because they have been cruel to him.

   a. What form of poetry is this?

   b. What do you notice about the poem's metre and rhyme scheme?

   c. What form do the last two lines take?

   d. How might the form of the last two lines affect the poem?

   e. How might the form of the whole poem emphasise the poet's meaning?

Poetry Anthology: Themes

You need to have a thorough understanding of your anthology poems and the different themes that they present.

Re-read the Poems

You will have studied a selection of modern and heritage poems based around a broad theme like Love and Relationships, Power and Conflict, Youth and Age, or Time and Place. The first thing you need to do is re-read your poems on a regular basis so they are familiar to you.

Group the Poems

Within the broad theme of the poems you have studied, there will be several smaller themes. You need to understand what these sub-themes are. For example:

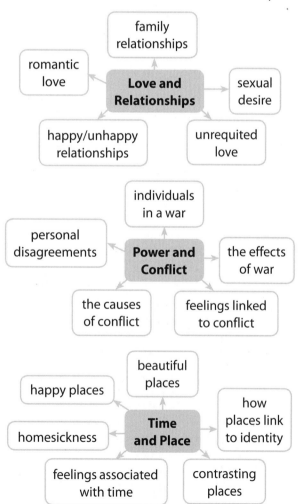

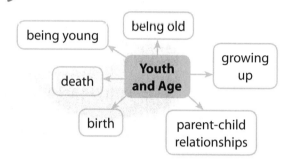

You then need to secure your understanding of which poems link to each sub-theme. Remember that a poem could contain more than one theme. For example:

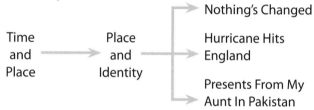

Language, Structure and Form

Once you have grouped your poems together by sub-theme, you need to think about the different techniques that they use to convey that theme. For example:

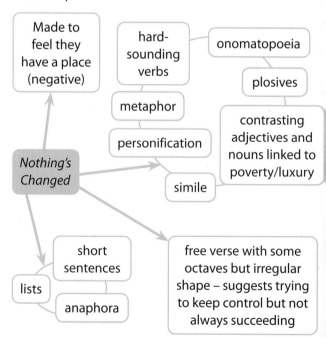

Read these sample sentence openers before attempting the Exam Practice question.

The poem _____ by _____ explores the theme of _____.

One of the key language features used to convey this theme is _____. We can see this in the line _____. Here, the poet uses _____ to suggest…

The poet adds to this by…

The poet also makes use of _____ in the line _____. Here the poet presents the theme of _____ by…

The poet develops this by…

The poet uses different structural devices to explore the theme of _____. In the line _____, the poet uses _____ in order to…

As well as this, the poet uses _____ in the line _____. The structure emphasises the ideas of the poem by…

The poet also uses the form of the poem to explore the theme of _____. By using _____ the poet…

SUMMARY

● Make sure you have re-read the poems from the section of the anthology that you have studied several times.

● Group them into sub-themes, remembering that a poem can contain more than one theme.

● Make sure you know what techniques each poem uses to convey each sub-theme.

● Practise writing about how different techniques convey meaning.

QUESTIONS

QUICK TEST

1. What are the sub-themes of the section of the anthology that you have studied?

2. Which poems link to each of your sub-themes?

3. What are the three areas of a poem that you should analyse?

EXAM PRACTICE

1. **EXTRA PRACTICE** *Using the sentence openers opposite, spend up to 30 minutes practising writing about one of your poems. Remember to establish the specific sub-theme that you are exploring and to include:*
   ● *Language*
   ● *Structure*
   ● *Form*   *[18 marks]*

Poetry Anthology: Comparison

You need to be able to compare how two poets use language, structure and form to explore the same theme.

Where to Start?

In the previous section, you identified the sub-themes of your anthology poems. You then matched different poems to the sub-themes. Finally, you identified the different features that individual poems used to present each sub-theme.

From here, you can start identifying similarities and differences in the use of language, structure and form to present a sub-theme. For example:

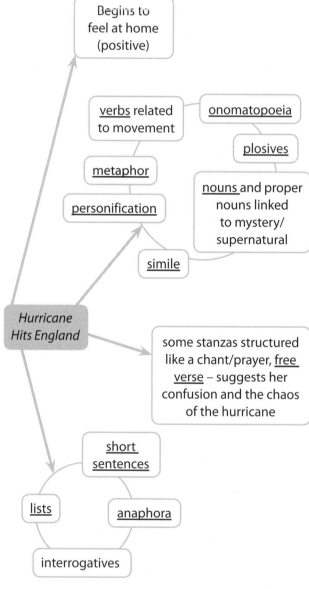

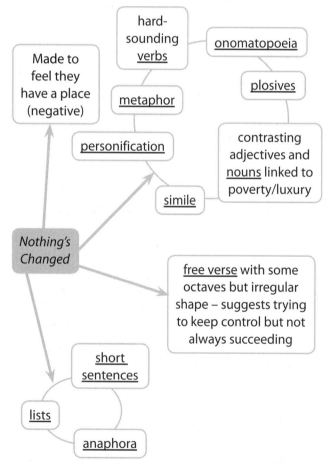

Organising Comparison and Analysis

Try to learn a simple pattern that you can follow when comparing two poems. For example:

1. State the theme you are exploring and which two poems you are using.
   For example: Nothing's Changed *and* Hurricane Hits England *both explore how places are linked to people's identities.*

2. Select a language feature that both poems use to explore your theme.
   For example: Both poets make powerful use of metaphors.

3. Say how Poem A uses the technique specifically to explore and provide a quotation as evidence.
   For example: In Nothing's Changed *the poet uses metaphor to show how the place affects the boy's emotions and behaviour, 'Hands burn / for a stone, a bomb, / to shiver down the glass'.*

4. Analyse how the language in your quotation gets across your idea. Consider developing your analysis by commenting on any effects of structure.
   For example: The image of burning is a metaphor for the anger that the boy feels. By using the verb 'burn' the poet shows the boy's wish to destroy the building but also indicates that these feelings are self-destructive. The poet emphasises this with the short list that shows the severity of the boy's weapons increasing as he gets older.

5. Use a connective of comparison to introduce Poem B, state what the technique is specifically exploring, and give a quotation as evidence.
   For example: Similarly, in Hurricane Hits England, *the poet uses metaphor to show how place affects emotions, 'Come to break the frozen lake in me'.*

6. Analyse how the language in your quotation gets across your idea. Consider developing your analysis by commenting on any effects of structure.
   For example: The 'frozen lake' metaphor is used to suggest how the poet does not feel emotionally attached to England. It suggests discomfort instead of feeling part of the country. However, the use of the verb 'break' shows that the hurricane is changing all this: the bad feelings are being destroyed and she is feeling more at home.

- Keep repeating stages 2–6 until you have analysed the language fully. Often you will find lots of similarities of technique but you can also contrast techniques (for example, one uses metaphor whilst the other uses simile).
- Once you have completed your sections on language, repeat stages 2–6 for any features of structure that you haven't already explored.
- Then repeat stages 2–6 to explore the form of each poem.

SUMMARY

- **Make mind-maps for each of the poems in your sub-themes, showing the different techniques that are used to convey the poet's ideas.**

- **Follow a simple pattern for comparing poems, remembering to include language, structure, and form.**

- **Try to focus your comparison on different techniques rather than ideas, as this will force you to analyse.**

QUESTIONS

QUICK TEST

1. Once you have stated an idea about a poem, what do you need to include as evidence?

2. What must you always do with this evidence before you move on to your next point?

3. What should you use to link your ideas about the two poems?

EXAM PRACTICE

1. **EXTRA PRACTICE** *Select one of the sub-themes from the section of the anthology that you have studied. Spend 45 minutes comparing how two poems from your anthology present that theme.*
   [36 marks]

Analysing Unseen Poetry

As well as writing essays about the poems that you have studied in class, you need to be able to analyse a poem that is new to you.

Have a Method

In order to analyse a poem without any help, you need to have a clear method to follow. This will keep you focussed and make sure that you analyse the three key elements of language, structure, and form.

If you have learned a method in class that you are happy with, practise applying it to the poem *The Echoing Green*. If you haven't learned a method yet, try Theme, Images, Form, Structure (TIFS):

- **T**heme
  The exam question usually gives you a theme to focus on. Read the poem, specifically looking for examples of that theme (you could underline key phrases). If the exam question is more general, read the poem carefully and identify its main ideas.
- **I**mages
  Staying focussed on the poem's theme, look at the language. What images help to get the theme across: verbs, adverbs, adjectives, simile, metaphor, personification, etc.?
- **F**orm
  How does the shape and form of the poem reflect or emphasise the poem's theme?
- **S**tructure
  What sentence types and punctuation are used to emphasise the poem's theme?

If the exam paper gives you a theme to explore, it is important that you stick to it. Students often fall into the trap of simply writing everything that they can work out about a poem. Keep focussed!

Using TIFS

Look at the poem, *The Echoing Green*, on page 59. If the examiner asks how the poem presents feelings of happiness, you might pick out, using TIFS, the following things:

- Images
  Personification of skies and bells as happy; metaphor ('laugh away care'); happy verbs (ring, welcome, sing, laugh); simile for happy family ('like birds in their nest'); relaxing image of old people ('sitting under the oak').
- Form
  Short lines, regular metre of five or six syllables, and rhyming couplets make it like a (happy) song. The uniform shape of the three stanzas could reflect the protection and safety shown in the last stanza.
- Structure
  Quite short sentences suggest the happy simplicity of being young and innocent; repeating words from stanza 1 in stanza 2 highlight happy ideas but also suggest a cycle – in the morning, they get up and the whole day is spent happily until it is bedtime.

You might begin:
One way in which the poet presents happiness is through personification, 'The sun does arise / And make happy the skies. / The merry bells ring'. This image of dawn uses personification to suggest that daytime is full of life and positivity. It seems to affect everything around (the bells), with onomatopoeia emphasising the cheerfulness. The fact that dawn is a daily occurrence also suggests every day is happy.

This atmosphere of happiness is also created through the poet's use of verbs…

The Echoing Green by William Blake

The sun does arise,
And make happy the skies.
The merry bells ring
To welcome the spring.
The skylark and thrush,
The birds of the bush,
Sing louder around,
To the bells' cheerful sound,
While our sports shall be seen
On the echoing green.

Old John with white hair
Does laugh away care,
Sitting under the oak,
Among the old folk.
They laugh at our play,
And soon they all say:
'Such, such were the joys
When we all, girls and boys,
In our youth-time were seen
On the echoing green.'

Till the little ones weary
No more can be merry;
The sun does descend,
And our sports have an end.
Round the laps of their mother
Many sisters and brothers,
Like birds in their nest,
Are ready for rest;
And sport no more seen
On the darkening green.

I Love To See The Summer by John Clare

I love to see the summer beaming forth
And white wool sack clouds sailing to the north
I love to see the wild flowers come again
And mare blobs* stain with gold the meadow drain
And water lilies whiten on the floods
Where reed clumps rustle like a wind shook wood
Where from her hiding place the Moor Hen pushes
And seeks her flag nest floating in bull rushes
I like the willow leaning half way o'er
The clear deep lake to stand upon its shore
I love the hay grass when the flower head swings
To summer winds and insects happy wings
That sport about the meadow the bright day
And see bright beetles in the clear lake play

*mare blobs = small, bright yellow flowers

SUMMARY

- Use TIFS, or your own method, to analyse unseen poetry.

- Focus on the main theme – do not just write everything you notice about the poem.

- Make sure that you analyse – do not just spot features; say how they affect the meaning of the poem.

- Remember to use specific terminology (such as metaphor, rhetorical question, or rhyming couplet).

QUESTIONS

QUICK TEST

1. What does TIFS stand for?

2. Why is the 'theme' aspect so important?

3. What must you do each time you spot a technique in the poem?

EXAM PRACTICE

1. **EXTRA PRACTICE** *Spend 30 minutes answering this question:*

How does John Clare convey his enjoyment of the summer in *I Love To See The Summer*?   [18 marks]

Comparing Unseen Poetry

As well as being able to analyse a previously unseen poem, you must be able to compare it to another poem (either unseen or from your anthology).

TIFS

Whatever method you used for analysing a single unseen poem, you should use it again when comparing two poems.

Make sure you have a clear understanding of the theme in the poems (it will usually be the same theme), then write sections that compare images, form and structure.

Quick Plan

You do not have time to create a huge mind-map of the two poems, so just do a quick plan in order to organise your ideas. One simple format is a Venn diagram, allowing you to visualise similarities and differences. Another planning method that some students find useful is simply to take a pen that has different colours into the exam: use one colour to underline key images, another to make notes on form, and another to pick out features of structure.

Ideas

Look back at the two poems on the previous page, *The Echoing Green* and *I Love To See The Summer*. If you were asked to compare how the two poems present nature, you might come up with the following ideas:

Echoing Green

Quite short sentences – the simplicity of nature

Similarities

Personification to make nature seem happy

Metaphor for nature being calming/beautiful

Verbs for happiness/peacefulness

Relaxing images

Anaphora: Blake uses it to suggest nature is important but at risk/ Clare uses it to emphasise his love of nature.

Rhyming couplets – like a song

I Love To See The Summer

Alliteration to emphasise beauty of nature

Written as one continuous sentence (with no end full stop) to show nature as one continuous whole.

Repetition of 'and' and list form to build up the wonders of nature.

Sonnet – love poem

Connectives

Whenever you are comparing poems, ensure you make use of connectives that suggest similarity or difference. For example: in comparison, similarly, just as, this can also be seen, in contrast, whereas, however, whilst.

You might write:

[1]*Both poets use metaphor in their presentation of nature.* [2]*Blake uses it to present nature as relaxing, 'Old John with white hair / Does laugh away care, / Sitting under the oak'.* [3]*The metaphor suggests that, when surrounded by nature, you can get rid of all your worries.* [4]*The verb 'laugh' is used to make this sound a particularly easy thing to do.* [5]*In comparison,* [6]*Clare uses metaphors to present the beauty of nature, 'mare blobs stain with gold the meadow'.* [7]*The idea that the yellow petals make the meadow look golden is very powerful, showing the positive reaction Clare has had to the flowers.* [8]*By choosing the word 'gold', Clare is also showing that he really values nature: these simply named 'mare blobs' are worth a great deal to him.*

1. Point of comparison focussed on the essay's theme
2. Idea about Poem A plus quotation as evidence
3. Analysis of Poem A
4. Development of analysis by commenting on more than one detail
5. Connective of comparison
6. Idea about Poem B plus quotation as evidence
7. Analysis of Poem B
8. Development of analysis by commenting on more than one detail

The two poets structure their poems differently to suggest different things about nature. Blake uses quite short sentences, 'The merry bells ring / To welcome the spring'. This simplicity reflects Blake's view that nature is simple; it is the lack of complexity that makes it so happy and enjoyable. In contrast, Clare's poem is one continuous sentence which doesn't even end with a full stop, 'And see bright beetles in the clear lake play'. This creates a big list that builds up all the things that Clare thinks make nature wonderful (clouds, flowers, animals, trees, insects, etc.). It also creates an idea that nature is a continuous cycle, which is why it doesn't end with a full stop.

SUMMARY

- When comparing poems, remember to cover TIFS: theme, images, form and structure.
- Prepare a quick planning method that works for you, such as a Venn diagram or multi-coloured pens.
- Remember to use connectives to make it clear that you are comparing.

QUESTIONS

QUICK TEST

1. What three aspects of a poem should you compare?
2. Why do you need to use connectives?
3. Look at the example of structure being compared (left). Can you identify a clear point of comparison, quotation plus analysis for the first poem, a connective, and quotation plus analysis for the second poem?

EXAM PRACTICE

EXTRA PRACTICE *Spend 40 minutes completing one of the tasks below.*

1. Look at the poems on the next two pages, *First Love* and *A Birthday*. Compare how the two poets present feelings associated with falling in love. [36 marks]

2. Look at the poem *A Birthday*. Compare how this poem and one from your anthology present feelings of being in love. [36 marks]

3. Look at the poem *First Love*. Compare how this poem and one from your anthology present the innocence of youth. [36 marks]

First Love

by Brian Patten

Falling in love was like falling down the stairs

Each stair had her name on it

And he went bouncing down each one like a tongue-tied lunatic

One day of loving her was an ordinary year

He transformed her into what he wanted

And the scent from her

Was the best scent in the world

Fifteen he was fifteen

Each night he dreamed of her

Each day he telephoned her

Each day was unfamiliar

Scary even

And the fear of her going weighed on him like a stone

And when he could not see her for two nights running

It seemed a century had passed

And meeting her and staring at her face

He knew he would feel as he did forever

Hopelessly in love

Sick with it

And not even knowing her second name yet

It was the first time

The best time

A time that would last forever

Because it was new

Because he was ignorant it could ever end

It was endless

A Birthday

by Christina Rossetti

My heart is like a singing bird
  Whose nest is in a water'd shoot;
My heart is like an apple-tree
  Whose boughs are bent with thickset fruit;
My heart is like a rainbow shell
  That paddles in a halcyon sea;
My heart is gladder than all these
  Because my love is come to me.

Raise me a dais of silk and down;
  Hang it with vair* and purple dyes;
Carve it in doves and pomegranates,
  And peacocks with a hundred eyes;
Work it in gold and silver grapes,
  In leaves and silver fleurs-de-lys*;
Because the birthday of my life
  Is come, my love is come to me.

*vair = a pattern used in heraldry (a rich family's coat of arms)
*fleur-de-lys = a decorative drawing or engraving of a lily (also used in heraldry)

Shakespeare: Character

You need to be able to comment on what characters are like and how Shakespeare shows this to his audience.

Who are the Main Characters?

The simplest way to start your revision is to make mind-maps or profiles of the different characters in the play that you have studied.

Put each character on a separate sheet and consider:

● Who are they?
● What key events are they involved with?
● What key relationships do they have with other characters?

> **Example**
> *Romeo and Juliet*
> *The Nurse*
> *Works for the Capulets and has nursed Juliet all her life.*
> *Has a close bond with Juliet*
> *Encourages Juliet to meet a man, reveals Romeo's identity, helps to arrange the marriage, tries to stop Lord Capulet's attack on Juliet, advises Juliet to marry Paris.*

What are They Like?

You should then add to your character notes what each one is like when we first meet them in the play. Think about their characteristics, thoughts, feelings, attitudes, and behaviour. It is also important to consider what others say about them.

> **Example**
> *The Nurse*
> *Old and funny (often in a bawdy way)*
> *Talks a lot and repeats herself*
> *Cares for Juliet*
> *Has a more relaxed relationship with Juliet than her mother does*
> *Loyal to Juliet*
> *Thinks love is physical and temporary*

What Evidence Do you Have?

For all of your ideas about your characters, you should support them with quotations. Include what act and scene your quotations are from to help you remember when different things take place.

> **Example**
> *Old – 'to my teeth be it spoken, I have but four' (Act 1, Scene 3)*
> *Funny (often in a bawdy way) – 'No less! nay, bigger; women grow by men.' (Act 1, Scene 3)*

How has Shakespeare Presented Character?

When making your character sheets, quickly pick out any specific features of language or structure within your quotations.

> **Example**
> *'No less! nay, bigger; women grow by men'*
> *[contrast, comparative adjective, metaphor, double meaning/innuendo]*

When your sheets are complete, you can also practise writing short paragraphs about each of your characters, including a point, some evidence and analysis.

> **Example**
> *The Nurse is presented as bawdily funny, 'No less! nay, bigger; women grow by men'. She creates a sexual joke by contradicting Lady Capulet's words with the comparative adjective 'bigger'. She is suggesting that women better themselves through marriage but turns this into a sexual innuendo with the metaphor 'women grow by men' being a double meaning for pregnancy.*

Read the extract from the Shakespeare play you have studied.

Julius Caesar (Act 1, Scene 2)

BRUTUS: If it be aught toward the general good,
        Set honour in one eye, and death i'th' other,
        And I will look on both indifferently,

Macbeth (Act 1, Scene 5)

LADY MACBETH: Hie thee hither,
        That I may pour my spirits in thine ear,
        And chastise with the valour of my tongue
        All that impedes thee from the golden round,

Much Ado About Nothing (Act 1, Scene 1)

BEATRICE: O Lord, he will hang upon him like a
        disease; he is sooner caught than the
        pestilence, and the taker runs presently
        mad. God help the noble Claudio!

Romeo and Juliet (Act 1, Scene 2)

LORD CAPULET: The earth hath swallow'd all my
        hopes but she;
        She is the hopeful lady of my earth:
        But woo her, gentle Paris, get her heart,
        My will to her consent is but a part;

The Tempest (Act 1, Scene 2)

ARIEL: Is there more toil? Since thou dost give
        me pains,
        Let me remember thee what thou hast
        promised,

The Merchant of Venice (Act 1, Scene 1)

BASSANIO: In Belmont is a lady richly left,
        And she is fair, and (fairer than that word),
        Of wondrous virtues,

Twelfth Night (Act 1, Scene 1)

DUKE ORSINO: That instant was I turn'd into a hart,
        And my desires, like fell and cruel hounds,
        E'er since pursue me.

SUMMARY

- Make sure you know who the main characters are in the play you are studying.

- Think about what they are like at the start of the play and where you have evidence for this.

- Practise analysing how key quotations reveal character.

QUESTIONS

QUICK TEST

1. Look at the extract opposite from the play you have studied. Analyse what the quotation shows about the character who is speaking and how this is achieved.

2. Find a different quotation from the play that shows the same thing about the character.

3. Using the quotation you selected for question 2, analyse how Shakespeare has used language or structure to convey meaning.

EXAM PRACTICE

Spend 5 minutes planning an answer to this question.

1. Choose one of the main characters from the play you have studied.

   Choose a scene from the first half of the play in which your chosen character features prominently. Select one page from that scene and analyse how Shakespeare presents the character.

   EXTRA PRACTICE *Spend 30 minutes turning your plan into a full exam response.* [36 marks]

Shakespeare: Character Development

Once you have established what characters are like, you need to think about how they develop.

Changes

Go back to your character sheets and add extra detail to them by considering how each of your characters is developed by Shakespeare. Think about start, middle and end.

Sometimes this will be an obvious change, such as falling in love, going mad, or becoming a better or worse person. The character might even die! However, it could just be that certain characteristics are emphasised such as someone's honesty or aggression.

Quotations and Analysis

Along with your extra notes, as before, add key quotations and highlight any specific features of language or structure that Shakespeare is using. This will help you to write paragraphs where you comment on how a character develops.

For example, you might write:
At the start of the play, Macbeth is respected as a great soldier, 'What he hath lost, noble Macbeth hath won'. The adjective 'noble' shows Macbeth is highly regarded and this is heightened by the fact that these are the words of the King. The contrasting verbs 'lost/won' present Macbeth as a victor but also someone receiving deserved honour. This is emphasised by how he is being compared with the dishonourable Thane of Cawdor and is being given his title.

However, by Act 4, Shakespeare's contrasting language shows that Macbeth is now hated for the way he rules Scotland, 'This tyrant, whose sole name blisters our tongues / Was once thought honest'. The use of the past tense in 'once thought' shows how Macbeth has lost people's respect and this is also seen in the word 'tyrant'. Shakespeare highlights this with the powerful metaphor which links Macbeth to an infection and suggests people are disgusted to even say his name.

Remember it's a Play!

When you are exploring Shakespeare's presentation of character, you should also try to respond to the form of the text (the fact that it is a play, not a novel or a poem).

Are there any specific dramatic devices, used to reveal information about character, that you can add to your character sheets?

Think about:
- asides and soliloquy (when a character speaks their thoughts aloud and only the audience is supposed to hear)
- dramatic irony (when we know something a character on stage does not)
- stage directions, such as characters concealing themselves to watch others
- **symbolic** 'props'
- do they speak in rhyming verse, blank verse, or prose (and is this relevant)?

Read the extract from the Shakespeare play you have studied.

Julius Caesar **(Act 3, Scene 1)**
BRUTUS: So are we Caesar's friends that have abridged
His time of fearing death. Stoop, Romans, stoop,
And let us bathe our hands in Caesar's blood
Up to the elbows and besmear our swords.

Macbeth **(Act 5, Scene 1)**
LADY MACBETH: Here's the smell of the blood still: all the perfumes of Arabia will not sweeten this little hand. Oh! oh! oh!

Much Ado About Nothing **(Act 3, Scene 1)**
BEATRICE: Contempt, farewell, and maiden pride, adieu!
No glory lives behind the back of such.
And, Benedick, love on; I will requite thee,
Taming my wild heart to thy loving hand.

Romeo and Juliet **(Act 3, Scene 5)**
LORD CAPULET: Hang thee, young baggage! disobedient wretch!
I tell thee what – get thee to church o' Thursday
Or never after look me in the face.

The Tempest **(Act 4, Scene 1)**
ARIEL: What would my potent master? Here I am.
[…] Thy thoughts I cleave to. What's thy pleasure?

The Merchant of Venice **(Act 3, Scene 2)**
BASSANIO: Madam, you have bereft me of all words,
Only my blood speaks to you in my veins,

Twelfth Night **(Act 5, Scene 1)**
DUKE ORSINO: You uncivil lady,
To whose ingrate and unauspicious altars
My soul the faithfull'st off'rings hath breath'd out
That e'er devotion tender'd – What shall I do?

SUMMARY

- Consider how your characters change or develop as the play progresses.
- Pick out key quotations that make these changes clear.
- As well as language and sentence structure, does Shakespeare use any dramatic devices to reveal character?

QUESTIONS

QUICK TEST

1. Look at the extract opposite from the play you have studied. It is linked to the extract you explored on page 65. Analyse how the quotation shows Shakespeare's development of the character.

2. Find a different quotation from the play that shows the same thing about the character.

3. Using the quotation you selected for question 2, analyse how Shakespeare has used language or structure to convey meaning.

EXAM PRACTICE

Spend 5 minutes planning an answer to this question.

1. Look back at the character you chose to examine on page 65.

   Choose a scene from the second half of the play in which the same character features prominently. Select one page from that scene and analyse how Shakespeare presents the character, including any ways in which the character has developed.

EXTRA PRACTICE *Spend 30 minutes turning your plan into a full exam response.*   [36 marks]

Shakespeare: Themes and Context

You need to understand how Shakespeare explores different ideas and how the play is affected by its context.

Themes

To begin with, you need to know the different themes of the play you have studied.

> **Example** *Romeo and Juliet*
>
> Love, Parent–Child Relationships, Friendship, Conflict, Youth, Time, Fate, Truth and Lies, Tragedy

You then need to know which characters and events relate to each of your themes.

> **Example** *Much Ado About Nothing*
>
> Lies: Don Pedro, Claudio, and Leonato tricking Benedick into love (Act 2, Scene 3); Hero and Ursula tricking Beatrice into love (Act 3, Scene 1); Don John ruining Hero's name (Act 3, Scene 2/Act 3, Scene 3); faking Hero's death (Act 4, Scene 1); all the lies uncovered and resolved (Act 5).

Exploring Themes

Once you have a clear understanding of your themes, practise analysing how Shakespeare presents them.

> **Example** *The Tempest*
>
> Shakespeare presents the theme of control through Prospero's dominance over Ariel, 'I will rend an oak / And peg thee in his knotty entrails till / Thou hast howled away twelve winters'. In this threat, the verbs 'rend' and 'peg' show Prospero's magical powers. These sound aggressive which shows he is controlling Ariel through fear. The verb 'howled' emphasises the misery he could cause Ariel.

Context: Setting

You also need to understand how the presentation of characters and themes is affected by the contexts of the play.

To begin with, you should think about your play's setting: where, when, what types of people, and what beliefs the people hold.

> **Example** *Macbeth*
>
> 10th century Scotland; the Scottish Thanes and their families/servants; conflict (a time of battles and the strongest taking charge); superstition (witches); religion (the Divine Right of Kings, heaven and hell); gender roles (women have much lower social status and were seen as weaker).

You should then think about how these contexts affect the play. For example, with Lady Macbeth, considering gender roles at the time would allow you to explore how strong she is and how unusual her relationship is with Macbeth.

Other Contexts

As well as exploring the contexts in which the play is set, think about when the play was written. What ideas and attitudes in Shakespeare's time (around 1600) may have affected the play?

As well as this, consider how audiences now and then may respond differently to characters, themes or events. For example, you may think about the presentation and treatment of Shylock in *The Merchant of Venice*.

Read the extract from the Shakespeare play you have studied.

Julius Caesar (Act 1, Scene 2)

CAESAR: What say'st thou to me now? Speak once again.

SOOTHSAYER: Beware the ides of March.

CAESAR: He is a dreamer. Let us leave him. Pass.

Macbeth (Act 2, Scene 2)

MACBETH: But wherefore could not I pronounce 'Amen'?

I had most need of blessing, and 'Amen' Stuck in my throat.

LADY MACBETH: These deeds must not be thought After these ways; so, it will make us mad.

Much Ado About Nothing (Act 4, Scene 1)

CLAUDIO: O, what authority and show of truth
Can cunning sin cover itself withal!
Comes not that blood as modest evidence
To witness simple virtue? Would you not swear,
All you that see her, that she were a maid,
By these exterior shows? But she is none:
She knows the heat of a luxurious bed;
Her blush is guiltiness, not modesty.

Romeo and Juliet (Act 3, Scene 4)

LORD CAPULET: Sir Paris, I will make a
desperate tender
Of my child's love. I think she will be rul'd
In all respects by me; nay, more, I doubt it not.
Wife, go you to her ere you go to bed
Acquaint her here of my son Paris' love.

The Tempest (Act 5, Scene 1)

PROSPERO: Though with their high wrongs I am
struck to th' quick,
Yet with my nobler reason 'gainst my fury
Do I take part. The rarer action is
In virtue than in vengeance.

The Merchant of Venice (Act 2, Scene 5)

SHYLOCK: Hear you me Jessica,
Lock up my doors, and when you hear the drum
And the vile squealing of the wry-neck'd fife,
Clamber not you up to the casements then,
Nor thrust your head into the public street
To gaze on Christian fools with varnish'd faces,

Twelfth Night (Act 1, Scene 5)

OLIVIA: 'I am a gentleman.' I'll be sworn thou art:
Thy tongue, thy face, thy limbs, actions and spirit,
Do give thee five-fold blazon. Not too fast: soft! soft!
Unless the master were the man.

SUMMARY

- **Make sure you know the different themes of your play.**

- **Have a clear understanding of which characters and events are used to present each theme.**

- **Think about how different contexts (setting, Shakespeare's times, and changing audience response) affect Shakespeare's presentation of characters and themes.**

QUESTIONS

QUICK TEST

1. What are the different themes in the play you have studied?

2. What are the different contexts in the play you have studied?

3. Looking at the relevant quotation opposite, how does it show how context affects themes and character in the play you have studied?

EXAM PRACTICE

Using the list on page 92, select the extract and theme for the play you have studied. Then spend 5 minutes planning an answer to this question.

1. How does Shakespeare present the given theme in the stated extract? (Remember to include links to context where relevant.)

EXTRA PRACTICE *Spend 30 minutes turning your plan into a full exam response.* [36 marks]

Shakespeare: Learning Quotations

You need to be able to learn some quotations from the play you have studied.

Why?

In the exam, you will be given an extract to analyse and will need to link your ideas to other points in the play. In order to analyse Shakespeare's use of language and structure, you need to learn some useful quotations.

Step 1: Choose

Select 10 quotations that are multi-purpose. Ideally, they should feature your main characters, different themes, and features of language, structure and form.

Write them in big letters on a sheet of paper. Make sure it is clear who's speaking. Underneath, make a note of the Act/Scene, which theme it is exploring and what techniques it features.

If you know you struggle with memory, instead of trying 10 straight away, go for five or even three. Then repeat these steps another day and learn some more.

Step 2: Remove

Learning quotations is easier if you have some cue cards or even a mini white board. Rewrite your quotations (this is part of the learning process) but miss out two or three key words from each one.

Now test yourself by adding in the missing words, looking back at your original list to check you are right. This can be done aloud, in writing, or you can get someone to quiz you.

Step 3: Chunk

Rewrite your quotations again, remembering this is one of the ways they are fixing themselves in your head. This time, miss out a chunk.

You might allow yourself only the first two words, or the first and last words, or two words in the middle. If you have time, you could repeat this step three times by doing each of those arrangements.

Again, test yourself or get someone to test you.

Step 4: Recall

By now, you should have a fairly good recall of your quotations. This time, give your original list to the person helping you or write the speakers, themes and techniques of your quotations on different shuffled cue cards.

Now test yourself by coming up with the quotation that matches the character, theme, or technique that is on your cue card or is called out by your helper. If you get any wrong, try not to worry, just read or listen to the correct answer. Again, this is part of the learning process!

Step 5: Analyse

Repeat the task above but, this time, also comment on how specific features of language, structure or form are conveying ideas.

Step 6: Refresh

Try to recall your quotations over the next few days. Say them aloud on the bus, use them in practice essays, get your family to test you or create small quizzes amongst your friends.

Read the extract from the Shakespeare play you have studied.

Julius Caesar **(Act 1, Scene 2)**
BRUTUS: For let the gods so speed me as I love
           The name of honour more than I fear death.

Macbeth **(Act 3, Scene 2)**
MACBETH: O! full of scorpions is my mind, dear wife!

Much Ado About Nothing **(Act 1, Scene 1)**
BEATRICE: I wonder that you will still be talking,
            Signior Benedick: nobody marks you.
BENEDICK: What, my dear Lady Disdain! Are you
            yet living?

Romeo and Juliet **(Act 1, Scene 5)**
ROMEO: Did my heart love till now? Foreswear it, sight!
          For I ne'er saw true beauty till this night.

The Tempest **(Act 1, Scene 2)**
PROSPERO: Thou poisonous slave, got by the devil
             himself
             Upon thy wicked dam; come forth!

The Merchant of Venice **(Act 3, Scene 2)**
PORTIA: This house, these servants, and this
         same myself
         Are yours, – my lord's! – I give them with
         this ring.

Twelfth Night **(Act 1, Scene 4)**
VIOLA: I'll do my best
        To woo your lady: *[Aside]* yet, a barful strife!
        Whoe'er I woo, myself would be his wife.

SUMMARY

- Choose 'good', multi-purpose quotations that are more likely to be useful in the exam.
- Remove words and chunks to help you remember.
- Practise analysing your quotations.
- Regularly reinforce your memory at different points in the week.

QUESTIONS

QUICK TEST

1. Choose the quotation from the list opposite that matches the play you have studied. Say it aloud three times.

2. Cover the second half. Say it again three times, trying to get the end right.

3. Cover the first half. Say it again three times, trying to get the start right.

4. Cover it completely. Can you remember the whole quotation? Say it three times.

PRACTICE

1. Write a paragraph about the quotation that you learned in the Quick Test, analysing how it shows Shakespeare's use of language and/or structure to present character or theme.

Shakespeare: Working With and Beyond an Extract

You need to be able to answer the different parts of the Shakespeare exam question.

The Question

You will be given a theme or character to focus on. You cannot take your copy of the play into the exam. The question will come with an extract to get you started but you will also be expected to relate your ideas to two or three other scenes from the play.

For example:
How does Shakespeare present Beatrice's attitude towards Benedick? Refer to this extract from Act 1, Scene 1 and elsewhere in the play.

The Extract

The extract is there to help you, not trip you up! Use it to form clear ideas related to your focus. It is important that you keep to this focus rather than just telling the examiner everything you can work out about the extract.

Because you have been given an extract, the examiner will expect detailed analysis of how Shakespeare uses language, structure and form to convey meaning.

You must also include context. You do not need to do this for every point but you must get it in where you can.

Moving Beyond

Depending on your exam board, you will either write half your essay about the extract then your other half about the rest of the play, or you will analyse the extract and link each of your points to the rest of the play.

Whichever you are doing, keep focussed on the exam question and make clear links between different parts of the play to show that you understand how Shakespeare is developing his ideas.

Make sure you incorporate any relevant quotations that you have learned so you can continue to provide detailed analysis. However, don't just put in a quotation simply because you've learned it; it must fit the exam question and your ideas.

You may not always have a supporting quotation. Do not let this stop you from exploring how Shakespeare presents or develops his ideas. Just make a clear reference to the part of the play (such as: 'In Act 1 where Prospero repeatedly insults Caliban'). You should also remember that a quotation doesn't have to be long; even if you only remember a key word, put it in quotation marks and analyse it.

As with the extract, whenever you can, include comments about how the play is affected by context.

Example

To give you an idea of what your response might look like, read through the start of a student's essay that is printed opposite. Their question was:

How does Shakespeare present Lady Macbeth's villainy in this extract (Act 1, Scene 5, lines 38–73) and the rest of the play?

In the extract from Act 1, Scene 5, Shakespeare presents Lady Macbeth as a sly, devious villain, 'look like th'innocent flower, / But be the serpent under't'. The use of simile then metaphor shows she pretends to be nice but is really dangerous. This is emphasised by the change in sounds between the lines: soft l sounds changing to harsher plosives and sinister sibilance. The 'flower' is a typical image of femininity, suggesting she presents herself as conventionally meek and mild, whilst 'serpent' borrows biblical imagery from the Eden story to show she is a manipulative villain.

This manipulative side to her villainy is also seen later on, especially Act 1, Scene 7, where she convinces Macbeth to kill the king, 'What beast was't then, / That made you break this enterprise to me?'. Shakespeare gives her a rhetorical question to make Macbeth feel bad for changing his mind, and couples this with irony ('beast') to show her humiliating him and making him feel cowardly. The word 'enterprise' also shows her tempting Macbeth as it sounds like a business deal that they will benefit from. Her manipulative behaviour emphasises her villainy and this would have been particularly apparent in the 1600s when women were expected to be subservient to men.

In Act 1, Scene 5, Lady Macbeth is also made villainous in her soliloquy by linking her to the devil, 'pall thee in the dunnest smoke of Hell, / That my keen knife sees not the wound it makes'. As well as the reference to 'Hell', Shakespeare uses the superlative adjective 'dunnest' to suggest she wants to be the most evil possible. This may be linking to the Divine Right of Kings and her awareness that the murder is against nature and will damn her for eternity. Despite this, the link to funerals ('pall') and the double meaning of 'keen' (sharp and eager) shows that she really wants to kill the king.

Once they have killed the king, in Act 2, Scene 2, Lady Macbeth's devilish villainy is shown by her lack of conscience about what they have done…

SUMMARY

- Use the extract to come up with clear ideas. Keep focussed on the essay question.

- Make sure you analyse the language, structure and form of the extract in detail.

- Refer to two or three scenes from elsewhere in the play, making use of any quotations that you have learned or specific references to parts of a scene.

QUESTIONS

QUICK TEST

Look again at the sample answer.

1. Identify the two main points that are being made about Lady Macbeth's villainy.

2. What different features of language, structure and form has the student analysed?

3. What different aspects of context has the student considered? Are they about the setting of the play, the time Shakespeare was writing, or different audience responses?

EXAM PRACTICE

1. Choose the question from page 92 that relates to the play you have studied. Spend 10 minutes planning an answer.

EXTRA PRACTICE *Spend 60 minutes turning your plan into a full exam response.* [36 marks]

19th Century Prose: Character

You need to have a clear understanding of who the main characters are in the 19th century novel you have studied and how they are presented.

Who

As you did for your Shakespeare play, start by thinking about who each of your main characters are, what key events in the novel they are involved in, and what relationships they have with other characters.

> **Example**
> *The Strange Case of Dr Jekyll and Mr Hyde*
>
> Mr Hyde
>
> *Jekyll's dark side, released through a scientific experiment. Enters Jekyll's house by a side door.*
>
> *Trampling the child; meeting Utterson; the murder of Danvers Carew (and its later re-telling); Hyde's death (and its later re-telling as Jekyll's suicide); the transformations and their effect on Lanyon; Hyde taking control.*

What and Where

Once you know who your characters are and have revised where they appear, you should make notes on what they are like. Think about their characteristics, their behaviour, and their speech. Include their attitudes towards others, as well as what other characters think about them. You should also consider how far their character is reflected in their setting.

> **Example**
> Mr Hyde
>
> *Violent/aggressive; powerful; selfish; lack of guilt/conscience; sinful; repulses and frightens people*
>
> *The dark, sordid, side entrance of the house that Hyde uses, compared to the respectable entrance on the main street.*

Evidence

Add to your character notes by supporting all of your ideas with quotations. Include what chapter and page your quotations are from to help you remember when different things take place.

> **Example**
> *Mr Hyde*
>
> Powerful: *'It wasn't like a man; it was like some damned Juggernaut.'* (Chapter 1, page 5)

Analysis

Strengthen your revision by underlining key features of language and structure in your quotations.

> **Example**
> *'It wasn't like a man; it was like some damned Juggernaut.'*
>
> *[pronoun; short clauses; contrasting similes; powerful adjective; powerful noun]*

You could then practise writing short paragraphs about each of your characters, including a point, some evidence, and analysis.

> **Example**
> *Mr Hyde is presented as very powerful, 'It wasn't like a man; it was like some damned Juggernaut.' The pronoun 'it' suggests that Hyde's strength and behaviour make him seem unusual and inhuman, which is emphasised by the contrasting similes and the demonic implications of the adjective 'damned'. The use of the noun 'juggernaut' suggests uncontrollable force, like a large speeding vehicle, and the short clauses highlight Enfield's shock at Hyde's strength.*

Read the quotation from the novel you have studied before attempting the Quick Test questions.

The Strange Case of Dr Jekyll and Mr Hyde
Dr Jekyll: 'a large, well-made, smooth-faced man of fifty, with something of a slyish cast perhaps, but every mark of capacity and kindness.'

A Christmas Carol
Ebenezer Scrooge: 'Hard and sharp as flint, from which no steel had ever struck out generous fire; secret, and self-contained, and solitary as an oyster.'

Great Expectations
Abel Magwitch: 'A man who had been soaked in water, and smothered in mud, and lamed by stones, and cut by flints, and stung by nettles, and torn by briars;'

Jane Eyre
Jane Eyre: 'Why was I always suffering, always browbeaten, always accused, for ever condemned? Why could I never please? Why was it useless to try to win any one's favour?'

Frankenstein
Victor Frankenstein: 'The world was to me a secret which I desired to divine. Curiosity, earnest research to learn the hidden laws of nature, gladness akin to rapture, as they were unfolded to me, are among the earliest sensations I can remember.'

Pride and Prejudice
Mrs Bennet: 'She was a woman of mean understanding, little information, and uncertain temper… The business of her life was to get her daughters married; its solace was visiting and news.'

The Sign of Four
Sherlock Holmes: 'For some little time his eyes rested thoughtfully upon the sinewy forearm and wrist all dotted and scarred with innumerable puncture-marks.'

War of the Worlds
The narrator: 'I still believed that there were men in Mars. My mind ran fancifully on the possibilities of its containing manuscript, on the difficulties in translation that might arise, whether we should find coins and models in it, and so forth.'

Silas Marner
Silas Marner: ' "There is no just God that governs the earth righteously, but a God of lies, that bears witness against the innocent." '

SUMMARY

- Make sure you know who the main characters are in the novel you are studying.

- Think about what they are like at the start of the novel and where you have evidence for this.

- Practise analysing how key quotations reveal character.

QUESTIONS

QUICK TEST

1. Look at the quotation opposite from the novel you have studied. Analyse what the quotation shows about the character and how this is achieved.

2. Find a different quotation from the early sections of the novel that shows the same thing about the character.

3. Using the quotation you selected for question 2, analyse how the author has used language or structure to convey meaning.

EXAM PRACTICE

Spend 5 minutes planning an answer to this question.

1. Choose one of the main characters from the novel you have studied.

   Choose a page from the first half of the novel in which your chosen character features prominently. How does the author present the character at this point in the novel?

EXTRA PRACTICE *Spend 30 minutes turning your plan into a full, analytical exam response.*

[36 marks]

19th Century Prose: Character Development

Now you have revised what characters are like at the start of the novel, you should think about how they develop.

Changes

Add further detail to your character notes by considering how the author develops each of your characters. Think about start, middle, and end. Identify any key chapters that are turning points for characters.

Some changes will be obvious, such as becoming a better person, falling in love, or even dying. Sometimes a character will change more than once. However, it could also be that certain characteristics are simply emphasised such as someone's determination or their kindness.

Quotations and Analysis

As before, add key quotations to your new notes and highlight any specific features of language or structure that your author is using. This will help you to analyse specifically *how* a character develops.

Prose Devices

When you analyse quotations, you will be exploring language and structure. However, you should also think about whether the form of the text (the fact it is a novel, not a poem or play) is affecting the presentation of character.

Are there any specific features of prose that are used to reveal or emphasise information about character?

Think about:
- Is your novel first or third person?
- What other ways does the author convey information, such as dialogue, dual narrative, diaries or newspaper extracts?
- Is the novel structured in a linear way (chronological) or does it move back and forth between events?
- How do these different things affect your understanding of characters in the novel?

Example
You might write:
At the start of Great Expectations, *Dickens presents Pip as feeling close to Joe. This can be seen when he considers telling him the truth about the convict, 'I loved Joe,[…] The fear of losing Joe's confidence'. The powerful verb 'love' shows his strong feelings towards Joe. This is emphasised by the abstract noun 'fear' which shows how much Pip values, and would not want to lose, their close relationship.*

However, once Pip becomes a gentleman, he is increasingly ashamed and annoyed at Joe, 'I felt impatient of him and out of temper with him; in which condition he heaped coals of fire on my head.' The words 'impatient' and 'temper' contrast with his earlier affection. This is highlighted by the metaphor which suggests that every unsophisticated word and action (the coals symbolising Joe's humble life as a blacksmith) now angers Pip.

Read the quotation from the novel you have studied before attempting the Quick Test questions.

The Strange Case of Dr Jekyll and Mr Hyde

Mr Hyde: 'Evil… had left on that body an imprint of deformity and decay. And yet when I looked upon that ugly idol in the glass, I was conscious of no repugnance, rather of a leap of welcome.'

A Christmas Carol

Ebenezer Scrooge: 'He went to church, and walked about the streets…, and patted children on the head, and questioned beggars, and looked down into the kitchens of houses…, and found that everything could yield him pleasure.'

Great Expectations

Abel Magwitch: 'He grasped them heartily, raised them to his lips, kissed them, and still held them. "You acted noble, my boy," said he. "Noble, Pip!"'

Jane Eyre

Jane Eyre: 'My future husband was becoming to me my whole world; and more than the world: almost my hope of heaven.'

Frankenstein

Victor Frankenstein: 'I perceived… (sight tremendous and abhorred!) that it was the wretch whom I had created. I trembled with rage and horror,'

Pride and Prejudice

Mrs Bennet: 'He was received by Mrs. Bennet with a degree of civility which made her two daughters ashamed, especially when contrasted with the cold and ceremonious politeness of her curtsey and address to his friend. '

The Sign of Four

Sherlock Holmes: 'We both started in our chairs. There was Holmes sitting close to us with an air of quiet amusement. "Holmes!" I exclaimed. "You here! But where is the old man?"'

War of the Worlds

The narrator: 'In a flash I was after him. I was fierce with fear. Before he was halfway across the kitchen I had overtaken him. With one last touch of humanity I turned the blade back and struck him with the butt.'

Silas Marner

Silas Marner: ' "I've come to love her as myself, I've had light enough to trusten by; and now she says she'll never leave me, I think I shall trusten till I die."'

SUMMARY

- Consider how your characters change or develop as the novel progresses.

- Pick out key quotations that make these changes clear.

- As well as language and sentence structure, does the author use any specific features of prose to show things about characters?

QUESTIONS

QUICK TEST

1. Look at the extract opposite from the novel you have studied. It is linked to the extract you explored on page 75. Analyse how the quotation shows the author's development of the character.

2. Find a different quotation from the novel that shows the same thing about the character.

3. Using the quotation you selected for question 2, analyse how the author has used language or structure to convey meaning.

EXAM PRACTICE

Look back at the character you chose to examine on page 75. Spend 5 minutes planning an answer to this question.

1. Choose a page or two from later in the novel where the same character features prominently. Analyse how the author presents the character, including any ways in which the character has developed.

EXTRA PRACTICE *Spend 30 minutes turning your plan into a full exam response.* [36 marks]

19th Century Prose: Themes

You need to understand how different ideas are explored in the 19th century novel that you have studied.

Identifying Themes

You should begin by noting down the different themes in your novel. For example:

- *Pride and Prejudice*:
  Love, Marriage, Pride, Family, Class, Prejudice.
- *Jane Eyre*:
  Love, Heart vs Mind, Class, Social Rules, Gender Roles, Independence, Religion, Atonement.

You should then add details to your notes about which characters and events help to portray each theme. For example:

- *Pride and Prejudice*
  Pride: Elizabeth's pride in her ability to judge others; Darcy's pride in his social status; the way pride gets in the way of Elizabeth and Darcy's relationship; Elizabeth and Darcy overcoming their pride to find love.
- *Jane Eyre*
  Independence: Jane's dependency on others and its effect on her; Jane's attempts to free herself from dependency; Jane's independent mind contrasted with her work in service; Jane's refusal to marry St John River; Rochester's dependence on Jane towards the end of the novel.

Exploring Themes

With a clear understanding of your themes and where they appear in the novel, you can begin revising how they are presented.

Practise stating an idea about the theme, and linking it to characters or key events. Support your idea with a quotation and analyse how the language or structure in the quotation shows your idea. To develop your response, try to find a similar quotation that provides you with different techniques to analyse.

Example
A Christmas Carol

Dickens explores the theme of poverty when the Spirit presents Scrooge with the vision of Want and Ignorance, 'two children; wretched, abject, frightful, hideous, miserable. They knelt down at its feet, and clung upon the outside of its garment.' The use of children is designed to create sympathy from the reader. The list of adjectives builds up a description of the effects of poverty, showing how it brings unhappiness and fear whilst also implying that it disgusts others. Dickens's use of the verbs 'knelt' and 'clung' emphasises how the poor are desperate for help and protection. These words also relate to animal behaviour to show the poor are treated as lowly people who are less than human.

The effects of poverty are also explored through the Cratchit family…

Read the quotation from the novel you have studied before attempting the Quick Test and Exam Practice questions.

The Strange Case of Dr Jekyll and Mr Hyde
Respectability: ' "I was thinking of my own character, which this hateful business has rather exposed." '

A Christmas Carol
Selfishness: 'the clerk's fire was so very much smaller that it looked like one coal. But he couldn't replenish it, for Scrooge kept the coal-box in his own room;'

Great Expectations
Home: 'It is a most miserable thing to feel ashamed of home. There may be black ingratitude in the thing, and the punishment may be retributive.'

Jane Eyre
Class: ' "You have no business to take our books; you are a dependent, mama says; you have no money; your father left you none; you ought to beg, and not to live here with gentlemen's children like us," '

Frankenstein
Isolation: 'I longed to join them, but dared not. I remembered too well the treatment I had suffered the night before from the barbarous villagers,'

Pride and Prejudice
Marriage: ' "Single, my dear, to be sure! A single man of large fortune; four or five thousand a year. What a fine thing for our girls!" '

The Sign of Four
Danger: 'just behind where we had been standing, stuck one of those murderous darts which we knew so well… Holmes smiled at it and shrugged his shoulders…, but I confess that it turned me sick'

War of the Worlds
Fear: 'A sudden chill came over me. There was a loud shriek from a woman behind. I half turned, keeping my eyes fixed upon the cylinder still, from which other tentacles were now projecting,'

Silas Marner
Hopelessness: 'His life had reduced itself to the functions of weaving and hoarding, without any contemplation of an end towards which the functions tended.'

SUMMARY

- Make sure you know your novel's different themes.
- Have a clear understanding of which characters and events relate to each theme.
- Explore how language and structure are used to present themes.

QUESTIONS

QUICK TEST

1. What are the different themes in the novel you have studied?

2. Which do you think is the most central theme and why?

3. Looking at the relevant quotation opposite, how does it explore a theme in the novel you have studied?

EXAM PRACTICE

Spend 5 minutes planning an answer to this question.

1. How does your 19th century novelist present the theme of _____?

   Explore the theme for your novel that is given in the list opposite. You could use the quotation that you have already explored as a starting point.

   EXTRA PRACTICE *Spend 30 minutes turning your plan into a full exam response.* [36 marks]

19th Century Prose: Context

Your understanding of characters and themes should also be informed by the context of the novel.

What is Context?

Context can be defined as the circumstances that shape something. So the characters and themes in a novel will be shaped by when it was written, who wrote it, and when and where the novel is set. It is important to have a clear understanding of context if you are to understand the novel fully.

The 19th Century

The 19th century was a time of great change. Some of the century's most significant features are listed below. All of these will have shaped the writing of your novel in some way.

- Victorian values
  This term is often used to sum up life in the 19th century; it refers to a rigid code of social conduct, sexual restraint, and low tolerance of crime.
- Class
  Victorian society had a very clear class system. People didn't often come in contact with people from other classes. Things like marriage between classes were frowned upon.
- Social expectations
  The higher up in society you were, the more 'rules' there were about how you should live your life respectably and discreetly; this also seemed to increase prejudice about people 'below' them.
- Empire
  During the 19th century, the British Empire continued to grow, taking control of countries in order to make money from their natural resources and dominate world trade.
- Industrialisation
  Cities were growing, destroying the countryside as more factories were built. More and more people moved to cities to work, finding busy and polluted streets.

- Social problems
  Industrialisation made some people very rich but also led to much poverty. Lack of education, workhouses, drug abuse, child labour, prostitution, crime, disease, and homelessness became big issues that the Victorians were slow to tackle. The century is noted for the contrast between its social values and its social problems.
- Religion
  Despite Christian morality dominating society and its expectations, the Church did little to help tackle society's problems. This led to people starting to question religion more.
- Gender
  Men and women were far from equal. Legally and socially, men had more rights and greater freedoms. Women often needed to get married in order to live a comfortable life. Men were encouraged to be ambitious and work hard to become 'self-made men'.
- Science
  Research into germs and electricity changed the future, whilst the invention of motorcars, radio, and the theory of evolution began to change how humans behaved and viewed themselves.

Audience and Setting

It is worth considering how the original 19th century audience and a modern reader might respond differently to elements of the novel you have studied. We might be less shocked by Dr Jekyll's desires but more sympathetic to Miss Havisham's behaviour.

Depending on the novel's setting (what part of the country and what sections of society it features), the writer will have drawn on different elements of 19th century context. For example:

The Strange Case of Dr Jekyll and Mr Hyde
The main character and his alter ego need to be explored in relation to Victorian values.

A Christmas Carol
Scrooge's character mirrors the lack of compassion for society's problems amongst the richer people of the country.

Great Expectations
The 19th century class system helps us to understand the social prejudice of which Pip is both a victim and an offender.

Jane Eyre
Victorian values and attitudes to divorce help us to understand why Rochester is so keen to hide his past.

Frankenstein
The theory of evolution is vital to understanding Victor Frankenstein's behaviour.

Pride and Prejudice
Elizabeth Bennet challenges, and is a victim of, 19th century attitudes to gender.

The Sign of Four
Sherlock Holmes challenges social expectations through the contrast of his social status and his drug use.

The War of the Worlds
The horrors of the novel are highlighted by the scientific advances of the century and how primitive they still seem compared to the powers of the Martians.

Silas Marner
At the start of the novel, Silas's life in Lantern Yard reflects 19th century attitudes and events.

SUMMARY

- Learn the key contextual features of 19th century society.

- Have a clear understanding of which characters are affected by context.

- Think about how the main themes of the novel are linked to context.

QUESTIONS

QUICK TEST

1. What are the most important contextual features in the novel you have studied?

2. Which characters and themes do these contextual features affect?

3. Look at the list opposite. Find and learn a quotation that matches the point of context for your novel.

EXAM PRACTICE

1. Look again at the list opposite. Spend 10 minutes creating a mind-map of how the contextual feature that is listed for the novel you have studied matches the character or theme that is identified.

EXTRA PRACTICE *Spend 30 minutes turning your mind-map into an essay that proves the statement through evidence from the novel and analysis of language and structure.* **[36 marks]**

19th Century Prose: Working With and Beyond an Extract

In the exam you need to be able to explore an extract and comment on the novel as a whole.

The Question

As in the Shakespeare exam, you will be given a theme or character to focus on. The question will come with an extract to get you started; you will also be expected to relate your ideas to other parts of the novel but you cannot take your text into the exam.

For example:
How does Austen present Mr Wickham in Pride and Prejudice? *Refer to this extract from Chapter 16 and elsewhere in the play.*

The Extract

Use the extract to help you get started. Form clear ideas about the exam question. Avoid the temptation to just write generally about different things in the extract.

The examiner will expect detailed analysis of how language and structure convey meaning in the extract.

Although you do not need it for every point, you should also try to link your ideas to what you have learned about the 19th century context.

Moving Beyond

You can either write half your essay about the extract then your other half about the rest of the novel, or you can analyse the extract and link each of your points to the rest of the text. Whichever you choose, keep focussed on the exam question.

You will need to include relevant quotations so you can continue to provide detailed analysis. For help on learning key quotations, look back at pages 70–71. Don't just put in a quotation simply because you have learned it, though; it must fit the exam question.

If you cannot think of a quotation that supports what you want to write about, don't panic. Instead of missing your idea out of the essay, simply make a clear reference to the part of the novel (such as: 'In Chapter 1 where Jane is verbally and physically bullied by John Reed…'). You should also remember that a quotation doesn't have to be long; even if you only remember a key word, put it in quotation marks and analyse it.

As with the extract, whenever you can, include comments on how the novel is affected by its 19th century context.

To give you an idea of what your answer might look like, read through the start of a student's essay that is printed below. Their question was:

How does Dickens present Miss Havisham in this extract from Chapter 8 and the rest of the novel?

In Chapter 8, Miss Havisham is presented as mentally damaged by her past experiences when she talks about her heart, ' "Broken!" She uttered the word with an eager look, and with strong emphasis, and with a weird smile that had a kind of boast in it.' The adjective 'weird' suggests her madness. This is increased by the contrast between her exclaimed metaphorical description of what she has experienced ('Broken!') and the way she looks when she says it, with the 'eager look' and 'boast' foreshadowing her crazed desire to break Pip's heart.

We see this same demented cruelty in Chapter 12 when she whispers to Estella, ' "Break their hearts my pride and hope, break their hearts and have no mercy!" '. Dickens uses the same metaphorical image but twins this with several abstract nouns. Describing Estella as her 'pride and hope' shows that Havisham, in her crazed way, sees her cruelty and revenge as good, and this is heightened by her refusal of mercy. The rejection of the Christian morality that was at the centre of 19th century society is used to emphasise her presentation as unstable and villainous.

Chapter 8 also presents Miss Havisham as disturbing and manipulative, such as when she announces, ' "I have a sick fancy that I want to see some play." ' The sibilance in her speech creates a sinister atmosphere whilst the phrase 'sick fancy' shows that she is conscious of her madness and cruelty. The way she forces the two children to play is very creepy. This is increased by her double meaning of the word 'play', acknowledging that she is plotting against Pip, with Dickens using Pip's innocent first person voice to show that he is unaware of her second meaning.

Miss Havisham's manipulative nature can also be seen later in the novel when…

SUMMARY

- Use the extract to come up with clear ideas. Keep focussed on the essay question.

- Make sure you analyse the language and structure of the extract in detail.

- Refer to different points elsewhere in the novel, making use of any quotations that you have learned.

- Try to link your analysis to your understanding of the 19th century context.

QUESTIONS

QUICK TEST

Look again at the sample answer.

1. Identify the main points that are being made about Miss Havisham.

2. What different features of language, structure and form has the student analysed?

3. What different aspect of context has the student considered?

EXAM PRACTICE

1. Choose the question below that relates to the novel you have studied. Spend 10 minutes planning an answer.

EXTRA PRACTICE *Spend 60 minutes turning your plan into a full exam response.* [36 marks]

The Strange Case of Dr Jekyll and Mr Hyde
How does Stevenson present Dr Jekyll at the start of Chapter 3 and elsewhere in the novel?

A Christmas Carol
How does Dickens present Scrooge's attitude towards others at the start of Stave 1 and elsewhere in the novel?

Great Expectations
How does Dickens present social snobbery at the end of Chapter 8 and elsewhere in the novel?

Jane Eyre
How does Brontë present Jane's sense of independence at the start of Chapter 5 and elsewhere in the novel?

Frankenstein
How does Shelley create sympathy for the Creature at the end of Chapter 15 and elsewhere in the novel?

Pride and Prejudice
How does Austen present Jane's feelings for Mr Bingley at the start of Chapter 4 and elsewhere in the novel?

The Sign of Four
How does Doyle create an atmosphere of mystery at the end of Chapter 3 and elsewhere in the novel?

War of the Worlds
How does Wells make the Martians frightening at the end of Chapter 4 and elsewhere in the novel?

Silas Marner
How does Eliot present Silas Marner's relationship with Eppie at the end of Chapter 12 and elsewhere in the novel?

20th Century Texts: Character

You need to have a full understanding of what the characters in your modern text are like.

Who

As with your other literature texts, the first thing you should do when revising your modern text is establish who your characters are and what they are like at the start of the story. For example:

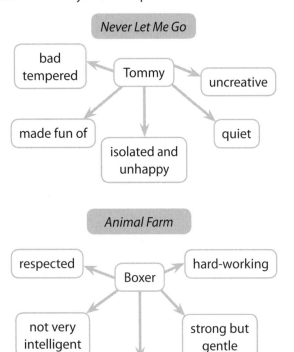

Evidence

Add quotations to your notes that prove your ideas.

> **Example**
> Boxer
>
> Dedicated: 'I will work harder!'
>
> Respected: 'he was universally respected for his steadiness of character and tremendous powers of work.'

You cannot take the text into the exam so try to choose memorable evidence that you might be able to learn. Notice that the second quotation in the previous example, although it is a bit long, is actually multi-purpose because it shows the character is respected but also refers to his strength and dedication.

Analysis

Practise turning your ideas and quotations into brief paragraphs of analysis.

> **Example**
> *One way in which George Orwell presents Boxer as dedicated to Animal Farm is through the motto that he repeats, ' "I will work harder!" ' The verb and adverb show that he is willing to do whatever he can to make the farm a success. Orwell's use of the exclamation mark and the **future tense** 'will' make this like a vow that Boxer is making to the farm.*

Background

You should also ask yourself how your characters fit into the context of the story.
- Are they typical characters for the time and place in which the story is set?
- Do they represent anything about history or society?
- Does the time and place in which the story is set affect the character in any way (such as their speech, their behaviour, or why things happen to them)?

> **Example**
> *Anita and Me*
>
> Mama: traditionally feminine but her wearing of trousers to work reflects the growing feminist movement of the 1970s; represents the hopes of Indian immigrants and the importance of family within their community; her place in Tollington and her expectations of Meena are based on her Punjabi heritage.

This is an extract of a student analysis based on the question below. Read it before attempting the Quick Test questions.

'How does JB Priestley present Mr Birling in *An Inspector Calls?'*

JB Priestley presents Mr Birling at the start of the play as an arrogant man who thinks he knows everything, 'And I'm talking as a hard-headed, practical man of business. And I say there isn't a chance of war'. This speech is a good example of the number of times Priestley has Mr Birling use the personal pronoun 'I' when he talks to show his sense of self-importance. This is emphasised here by the repetition of 'And' to show that he dominates conversations and has a lot to say about himself.

This can be seen elsewhere in his speech through the number of imperatives (like 'listen' and 'remember') that Priestley uses to show Birling thinks his words are important. The boastful adjectives 'hard-headed, practical' present him as strong and self-confident but we can also interpret this, in his context as an upper-middle class businessman focussed on making money, as uncaring.

Priestley also uses dramatic irony to show that Birling isn't as wise as he thinks: the play, set in 1912, was first performed in 1946 so there had been two world wars to prove him wrong. Such dramatic irony can also be seen later in his speech where he repeatedly describes the Titanic as unsinkable; the list of facts about its strength are used to suggest that he is unwittingly drawing a link between the ship and his own life.

QUESTIONS

QUICK TEST

Look at the extract of student analysis, opposite.

1. What different features of language and structure does the student pick out from their quotation to analyse?

2. Where has the student developed their analysis by linking their ideas to other parts of the text?

3. How has the student related characterisation to context?

EXAM PRACTICE

Spend 5 minutes planning an answer to this question.

1. Pick one of the main characters in your modern text. How are they presented in the first half of the story?

EXTRA PRACTICE *Spend 30 minutes turning your plan into a full, analytical exam response.*

[36 marks]

20th Century Texts: Character Development

You need to understand which characters change in your modern text, as well as how and why they change.

Development

Build up your character notes by considering how your main characters change. Do they become better or worse people, do their fortunes alter, do they change any of their ideas, do they survive the story?

As well as noting how they change, think about why they change. Are they affected by certain events or other characters? Is it a deliberate attempt to change, or natural progression? Is the story told over a short space of time or over several years?

> **Example**
> In Dennis Kelly's DNA, *Cathy starts off as someone who looks up to the leader of the group. As the play progresses, it is clear that she wants power. She becomes second in command and then, by the end of the play, the leader. As she gains more power, she becomes increasingly nasty.*

Evidence

As usual, you need to add evidence to your notes. Try to support your ideas with memorable key quotations as well as references to key events. Once you have some evidence, practise writing some analysis of how language and structure have been used to show changes in character.

> **Example**
> In Willy Russell's Blood Brothers, *Mickey is initially presented as lively and fun, 'Come on gang… let's go… [With an Indian call and arm wave]'. The two imperative verbs suggest Mickey's energy and this is emphasised by the childish play-acting in the stage direction. The way Russell gives him the words 'gang' and 'let's' also shows that Mickey enjoys being amongst company.*
>
> *However, later in the play his drug dependency leads him into depression: 'I can't cope with this. I'm not well. The doctor said, didn't he, I'm not well … I can't do things … leave me alone.' The repetition of the negative phrases 'I can't' and 'I'm not' make him seem defeated and inactive. The repeated use of the personal pronoun 'I', along with the request to be alone, also makes him seem self-absorbed and introverted, which is a contrast to his earlier friendliness.*

Form

Have you studied a modern play or novel? Remember to consider whether the development of characterisation has been emphasised through any features of form. For example:

Prose	Drama
First person or third person?	Stage directions: setting, props, lighting, music, actions, etc.
Structure: linear or non-linear? (How does this affect how character is shown?)	Structure: linear or non-linear? (How does this affect how character is shown?)
How is dialogue used to show character?	Who speaks the most/least and why?
Changes between chapters.	Changes between acts/scenes.

A possible analysis structure for exploring character development:

Topic sentence: state an idea about how the character changes/develops.

State what the character is like early in the story.

Support this with a reference to the text, ideally a quotation that contains lots of features to analyse.

Analyse how language, structure, and/or form has been used by the writer to present character.

Develop your analysis, either by linking your comments to another part of the text or by relating them to the context.

Using a connective, state how the character changes/develops.

Support this with a reference to the text, ideally a quotation that contains lots of features to analyse.

Analyse how language, structure, and/or form has been used to show development of character.

Develop your analysis, either by linking your comments to another part of the text or by relating them to the context.

QUESTIONS

QUICK TEST

1. Who are the main characters in your modern text?

2. Which characters change?

3. How and why do they change?

EXAM PRACTICE

Spend 5 minutes planning an answer to this question.

1. Pick one of the main characters in your modern text. How do they change?

EXTRA PRACTICE *Spend 45 minutes turning your plan into a full, analytical exam response.*

[36 marks]

20th Century Texts: Relationships and Importance

You need to apply your knowledge of characters to consider their importance and explore relationships.

Relationships

Develop your character notes by identifying which characters form relationships.

Decide what kind of relationship it is: friendly, romantic, criminal, unhealthy, etc?

Does the relationship stay the same or does it change during the story? For example, in *The History Boys,* Dakin's feelings for Irwin go from annoyance, to desperation to please, to attraction and flirtation.

Think about the different things that affect the relationship, such as events in the story, the passing of time, other characters, different backgrounds, etc.

Practise writing about how relationships develop.

> ### Example
> *At the start of* Lord of the Flies, *Piggy and Ralph do not have a strong relationship, ' "Sucks to your ass-mar!" '. Ralph focuses on his weakness by mockingly mispronouncing 'asthma'. This is also shown in the rudeness of 'Sucks to' and an exclamation mark to increase the tone of nastiness.*
>
> *Events on the island, such as the missing of the ship, strengthen their bond, 'Not even Ralph knew how a link between him and Jack had been snapped and fastened elsewhere.' The metaphor shows Ralph beginning to value Piggy more than Jack. The verbs 'snapped' and 'fastened' emphasise the importance of this.*

Importance or Significance

These are two key words that are sometimes used in the exam questions on the modern texts, such as: 'What is the significance of Squealer in *Animal Farm*?' or 'Do you think John Tate is an important character in *DNA*?'

If you are asked the significance or importance of a character, you need to consider the following things:
- How do they impact upon the story and affect other characters?
- How do they reflect the historical and social context of the story?
- How do they represent or explore different themes of the story? (For more on themes, see pages 90–91.)

Avoid falling into the trap of just writing generally about what you think of the character. You still need to come up with clear ideas, support them with evidence, and analyse how the writer's use of language, structure and form convey information.

For example, if you were writing about the significance of Squealer in *Animal Farm*, you might turn some of the following ideas into paragraphs of analysis:
- Squealer plays a key role in manipulating the other animals, through his speeches and the changing of the Commandments.
- He maintains support for Napoleon.
- A lot of his speeches reveal the growing inequality on Animal Farm.
- As Napoleon retreats from public life, Squealer becomes more prominent.
- He can be seen as representing Stalin's propaganda machine.

Read the sample question for the modern text you have studied before attempting the Exam Practice questions.

An Inspector Calls How does Priestley present the relationship between Mr Birling and his daughter, Sheila?

Hobson's Choice How does Brighouse present Hobson's relationship with his daughters?

Blood Brothers What is the significance of Eddie and Mickey's relationship?

Journey's End What is the significance of Trotter to the play?

Mother Said I Never Should How does Keatley present the relationship between Doris and Margaret?

DNA How does Kelly present the relationship between Cathy and Phil?

The History Boys Do you think the character of Posner is important to the play?

The Curious Incident of the Dog in the Night-Time How does Stephens present the relationship between Christopher and his father?

A Taste of Honey What is the significance of Geoffrey to the play?

Animal Farm Do you think the character of Benjamin is important to the novel?

Lord of the Flies What is the significance of Simon in the novel?

Anita and Me How does Syal present the relationship between Anita and her mother?

Never Let Me Go How does Ishiguro present the relationship between Ruth and Tommy?

Pigeon English How does Leman present the relationship between Harri and Dean?

The Woman In Black Do you think the character of Mr Jerome is important to the novel?

SUMMARY

- Make sure you know what the key relationships are in your modern text, as well as how and why they change or develop.

- Practise analysing how these things are shown by the writer.

- Think about the importance or significance of your characters to the text.

QUESTIONS

QUICK TEST

1. Which relationship in your text do you think is the most interesting and why?

2. What is the biggest thing in the story that affects this relationship?

3. Which character is most significant to the story and why?

EXAM PRACTICE

1. Select the exam question opposite that matches the modern text you have studied. Spend 5 minutes planning an answer to the question.

2. Substitute a different character or relationship for the one originally stated and spend another 5 minutes planning an answer to the new question you have created.

EXTRA PRACTICE *Spend 45 minutes turning one of your plans into a full, analytical exam response.*

[36 marks]

20th Century Texts: Themes

You need to understand how different ideas are explored in the modern text that you have studied.

Revise Context

Remind yourself of the time and place in which your story is set, as well as the different types of people or communities who are presented.

● What important ideas, socially (the way people live their lives) and historically (the events and attitudes of the time), appear in your story?
● Is the author using their story to say anything about the world as they see it?

Identifying Themes

Start by making a note of the different themes in your novel.

> **Example**
> *Never Let Me Go*
>
> Truth and lies; friendship; hopes and dreams; freedom; the past

Look at the list on page 91 and pick out the themes that are relevant to your text. Add any extra ones that you can think of to your notes, then start detailing which characters and events help to portray each theme.

> **Example**
> *Journey's End*
>
> Heroism: Raleigh's hero-worship of Stanhope; Stanhope's desperation to maintain his heroic image back home; Raleigh's patriotic image of a hero; Trotter as a different image of heroism.

Exploring Themes

Once you have a clear understanding of your themes and where they appear in the novel, you can start practising your analysis of how they are presented:

● State an idea about the theme, linking it to characters or key events.
● Support this with evidence from the text.
● Analyse how the language, structure or form shows your idea.
● Develop your paragraph by linking your ideas to the story's context or by finding a similar quotation that provides you with different techniques to analyse.

> **Example**
> *Animal Farm*
>
> *In* Animal Farm, *George Orwell uses the pigs to present the theme of inequality. We see this when Napoleon first takes charge and announces that all decisions will now be made by, 'a special committee of pigs, presided over by himself'. The adjective 'special' implies that the pigs are better than the other animals. The verb 'presided' links to the word 'presidential' and shows that, in contrast to the farm's ideals of 'comradeship' and equality, Napoleon is now their leader. This is added to by the way Orwell often refers to 'Napoleon himself', using the pronoun to create a sense of majesty. Working on their stereotypical image of greed, the pigs are used by Orwell to represent all governments who put themselves before their people but, specifically, the Stalinist regime in Soviet Russia. These inequalities increase through small events as the novel progresses, such as the pigs moving into the farmhouse and spending money on alcohol.*
>
> *The most significant point where the pigs present the theme of inequality is…*

Themes

Heroism

Courage and cowardice

Hopes and dreams

Friendship

Truth and lies

Freedom

Guilt and innocence

Love and sex

Equality

Parent-child relationships

Conflict

Class

Growing up

Knowledge

Personal problems

Leadership and power

Difference

Peer pressure

QUESTIONS

QUICK TEST

1. What are the different themes in the text you have studied?

2. Which do you think is the most significant theme and why?

3. How is that theme presented through character and events?

EXAM PRACTICE

Spend 5 minutes planning an answer to this question.

1. How does your modern text present the theme of _____?

   Choose one of the themes that you have identified as being central to the text you have studied.

   EXTRA PRACTICE *Spend 45 minutes turning your plan into a full exam response.* [36 marks]

Shakespeare: Themes and Context (p. 69)

EXAM PRACTICE (CONT.)

Julius Caesar: Manipulation in Act 3, Scene 2 (lines 69–117)
[*From:* PLEBEIAN: This Caesar was a tyrant.
To: PLEBEIAN: There's not a nobler man in Rome than Antony.]

Macbeth: Conscience in Act 1, Scene 7 (lines 1–44)
[*From:* MACBETH: If it were done, when 'tis done,
To: LADY MACBETH: Like the poor cat i'th'adage?]

Much Ado About Nothing: The battle of the sexes in Act 1, Scene 1 (lines 88–149)
[*From:* DON PEDRO: Good Signior Leonato, you are come to meet your trouble.
To: DON PEDRO: Your hand, Leonato; we will go together.]

Romeo and Juliet: Conflict in Act 3, Scene 1 (lines 35–95)
[*From:* BENVOLIO: By my head, here come the Capulets.
To: MERCUTIO: Go, villain, fetch a surgeon.]

The Tempest: Betrayal in Act 2, Scene 1 (lines 219–297)
[*From:* ANTONIO: I am more serious than my custom.
To: ANTONIO: To fall it on Gonzalo.]

The Merchant of Venice: Hatred in Act 1, Scene 3 (lines 35–115)
[*From:* BASSANIO: This is Signior Antonio.
To: SHYLOCK: What should I say to you?]

Twelfth Night: Love in Act 1, Scene 1 (lines 1–41)
[*From:* DUKE ORSINO: If music be the food of love, play on.
To: DUKE ORSINO: Love thoughts lie rich when canopied with bowers.]

Shakespeare: Working With and Beyond an Extract (p. 73)

EXAM PRACTICE (CONT.)

Julius Caesar
How does Shakespeare present the relationship between Brutus and Cassius in the extract (Act 1, Scene 2, lines 25–65) and the rest of the play?
[*From:* CASSIUS: Will you go see the order of the course?
To: BRUTUS: For that which is not in me?]

Macbeth
How does Shakespeare present the theme of madness in the extract (Act 2, Scene 1, lines 33–64) and the rest of the play?
[*From:* MACBETH: Is this a dagger, which I see before me,
To: MACBETH: That summons thee to Heaven, or to Hell.]

Much Ado About Nothing
How does Shakespeare present the character of Don John in the extract (Act 3, Scene 2, lines 71–105) and the rest of the play?
[*From:* DON JOHN: My lord and brother, God save you!
To: DON JOHN: It would better fit your honour to change your mind.]

Romeo and Juliet
How does Shakespeare present Romeo's attitude to love in the extract (Act 1, Scene 1, lines 161–196) and the rest of the play?
[*From:* BENVOLIO: What sadness lengthens Romeo's hours?
To: ROMEO: This is not Romeo, he's some other where.]

The Tempest
How does Shakespeare present the relationship between Ferdinand and Miranda in the extract (Act 1, Scene 2, lines 409–450) and the rest of the play?
[*From:* PROSPERO: The fringed curtains of thine eye advance,
To: PROSPERO: Soft, sir! one word more.]

The Merchant of Venice
How does Shakespeare present the theme of vengeance in the extract (Act 3, Scene 1, lines 39–66) and the rest of the play?
[*From:* SHYLOCK: There I have another bad match,
To: SHYLOCK: it shall go hard but I will better the instruction.]

Twelfth Night
How does Shakespeare present the character of Malvolio in the extract (Act 2, Scene 3, lines 87–123) and the rest of the play?
[*From:* MALVOLIO: My masters, are you mad?
To: MALVOLIO: She shall know of it, by this hand.]

Answers

Day 1

pages 4–5
Finding Information
QUICK TEST
1. a. Opinion
    b. Fact
2. Words like tree and types of trees, flower and types of flowers, animal and types of animals, etc.
3. To prove that you understand the text.

EXAM PRACTICE
1. Oblong; paths in the pattern of a Union Jack; majority of building more than one storey; three schools; there were hotels and boarding houses [**1 mark for each, up to a maximum of 3**]
2. Slugs and snails on the paths; the north-west wind; the damp bed; the feel of the bedspread [**1 mark for each, up to a maximum of 3**]
3. i, iv, vi [**1 mark for each**]
4. **1 mark** for a simple awareness of the weather;
    2–3 marks for identifying a few things about the weather and/or its effects, with some quotation as evidence;
    4–5 marks for a clear understanding of different things about the weather and its effects, with quotation as evidence;
    6 marks for a full understanding of the weather and its effects, well-supported by quotations.

pages 6–7
Language and Structure: Thoughts and Feelings
QUICK TEST
1. 'Exhausting' shows the trip was very tiring.
2. 'Surprisingly' shows the writer did not expect the party to be fun but was pleased that it was.
3. The simile shows the writer's nervousness was a strange, jittery, physical feeling in his stomach.

EXAM PRACTICE
1. a. 'good spirits', 'marvellously cheerful' or 'elation' [**1 mark for any**]
    b. A clear explanation of why the phrase suggests happiness, such as the positive adjective 'good', the adverb 'marvellously' or the adjective 'cheerful' suggesting a lot of happiness, or the noun 'elation' suggesting great happiness. [**1 mark for any**]
2. **1 mark** for a simple awareness of feelings;
    2–3 marks for identifying a few ways language shows feelings, with some quotation as evidence;
    4–5 marks for a clear understanding of how language shows different feelings, with quotation as evidence;
    6 marks for full understanding of how language shows different feelings, well-supported by quotations.

3. **1 mark** for a simple awareness of feelings;
    2–3 marks for identifying a few ways structure shows feelings, with some quotation as evidence;
    4–5 marks for a clear understanding of how structure shows different feelings, with quotation as evidence;
    6 marks for a full understanding of how structure shows different feelings, well-supported by quotations.

> *Avoid the temptation to simply note down all the different features or techniques that you can see; this is called feature-spotting and won't get you many marks. Only select the ones that relate to the question you have been set and always analyse their effect. This will then show your understanding of how language and structure work.*

pages 8–9
Language and Structure: Engagement
QUICK TEST
1. The short sentence summarises his feelings about the things described in the previous sentence. Or, the short sentence emphasises his positive view of his childhood.
2. Rhetorical question to get the reader to think/reflect on what they could do to reduce pollution and waste.
3. List to build up a sense of all the things that overwhelmed her about the shopping centre.

EXAM PRACTICE
1. **1 mark** for picking out a feature of language;
    1 mark for a relevant quotation;
    1 mark for an explanation of how it entertains.
    The idea must be from the first paragraph. e.g. The simile 'as difficult to conquer as the mountain peaks' is a humorous/over-the-top suggestion that Toblerones are really difficult to eat.
2. **1 mark** for picking out a feature of structure;
    1 mark for a relevant quotation;
    1 mark for an explanation of how it keeps the audience reading.
    The idea must be from the first paragraph. e.g. The writer ends the paragraph with a cliffhanger, 'lies a quietly classic piece of confectionery quite unlike any other.' The audience reads on to the next paragraph to find out exactly why the writer thinks Toblerone is so good and unique.
3. **1–3 marks** for a simple of awareness of why the text is engaging, with a few references to the text;
    4–6 marks for identifying several different ways in which the text is engaging, with some comment on use of language and/or structure, supported by some quotation;
    7–9 marks for a clear understanding of how the text has been made engaging through language and structure, with quotations as evidence;
    10–12 marks for a full analysis, well-supported by quotations, of how language and structure have been used to make the text engaging.

pages 10–11
Comparing Texts: Summarising Similarities and Differences

QUICK TEST
1. Gender, age, appearance, background, friends and family, job, feelings, behaviour, interests, etc.
2. Different colours; a table; a Venn diagram
3. Similarity – any two from: similarly, just as, the same, alike, equally, in common, likewise
   Difference – any two from: in contrast, however, whereas, is different, unlike, as opposed to, on the other hand

EXAM PRACTICE
1. Any three similarities, e.g. Both well-educated, both young, have an interest in music, read a lot, are not rich [**1 mark for each similarity, up to a maximum of 3; 1 mark for each supporting quotation, up to a maximum of 3**]
2. Any three differences, e.g. liked/disliked, sporty/not sporty, fun/not fun, sociable/unsociable, energetic/dull [**1 mark for each difference, up to a maximum of 3; 1 mark for each supporting quotation up to a maximum of 3**]

pages 12–13
Comparing Texts: How Ideas and Attitudes are Conveyed

QUICK TEST
1. 'What' just requires information to be taken from the text. 'How' requires analysis of the ways in which a writer conveys meaning.
2. Connectives of comparison
3. Language and structure

EXAM PRACTICE
1. **1–4 marks** for a simple awareness of their feelings about their writing, with a few references to both texts;

   5–8 marks for identifying several different feelings and trying to compare, as well as some comment on use of language and/or structure, supported by a quotation;
   9–12 marks for a clear understanding and comparison of how the writers show their feelings, with quotations as evidence;
   13–16 marks for a full analysis and comparison, well-supported by quotations, of how the writers show their feelings.

   Always spend time planning your answer by picking out the similarities and/or differences that you want to explore. This will help you to structure your response, maintain your focus, and ensure that you actually compare and analyse.

pages 14–17
Non-Fiction Exam Practice
Section 1
Text A
1. Fetch a recipe; take vegetables to neighbours; feed dogs, clean kennels; help with cow; collect vegetables [**1 mark for each, up to a maximum of 3**]
2. **1 mark** for a simple awareness of her time spent with Bob and Joan;
   2–3 marks for identifying a few things about life with Bob and Joan, with some quotation as evidence;
   4–5 marks for a clear understanding of the different things she felt and experienced whilst with Bob and Joan, with quotation as evidence;
   6 marks for a full understanding of different things she felt and experiences whilst with Bob and Joan, well-supported by quotations.

Text B
3. She blogs at Carrots and Kids; she runs a school gardening club; she has an allotment; she has five children; she lives in a village in the South Downs; she has had her allotment for seven years; she has a greenhouse and three raised vegetable beds at home; she drinks coffee [**1 mark for each, up to a maximum of 3**]
4. **1 mark** for a simple awareness of her attitude to gardening;
   2–3 marks for identifying a few things about her attitude to gardening, with some quotation as evidence;
   4–5 marks for a clear understanding of her different attitudes to gardening, with quotation as evidence;
   6 marks for a full understanding of her different attitudes to gardening, well-supported by quotations.

Text C
5. One brand is Heinz; tomato ketchup is red; Heinz ketchup was launched in 1876; it is based on 'catsup'; the original recipe contained tomatoes, cayenne, sugar, vinegar, cloves, and cinnamon; Heinz ketchup comes in a five-sided bottle [**1 mark for each, up to a maximum of 3**]
6. It is fun; it is sweet; it is not very spicy; it is thick; it is disappointing; Heinz tomato ketchup is the second most famous food product; the way it comes out of the bottle slowly is clever; it is essential to a meal [**1 mark for each, up to a maximum of 3**]
7. a, d, f [**1 mark for each**]

Section 2
Text A
1. **a.** Any suitable phrase, e.g. 'best of all', 'sniffing that air soaked with herbs', 'ripe, heavy, aromatic, scarlet tomatoes', 'the slow sleepy sound seducing you'
   b. Explain how one or more specific words or techniques show that she likes the garden. e.g. The list of positive adjectives shows she enjoys collecting the garden's produce.

2. **1 mark** for a simple awareness that she likes the garden;
2–3 marks for identifying a few ways language shows she likes the garden, with some quotation as evidence;
4–5 marks for a clear understanding of how language shows different things she likes about the garden, with quotation as evidence;
6 marks for a full understanding of how language shows different things she likes about the garden, well-supported by quotations.

3. **1–3 marks** for a simple awareness of her fears about the python;
4–6 marks for identifying a few ways language and/or structure show her fear of the python, with some quotation as evidence;
7–9 marks for a clear understanding of how language and structure show her fear about the python, with quotation as evidence;
10–12 marks for a full analysis of how language and structure show her fear about the python, well-supported by quotations.

Text B

4. **a.** Any suitable phrase, e.g. 'precious plot', 'pretty proud', 'my place', 'I escape here'
   b. Explain how one or more specific words or techniques show she is pleased with her allotment. e.g. the adjective 'precious' shows that the allotment is something she values highly.

5. **1 mark** for a simple awareness of pros and/or cons of an allotment;
2–3 marks for identifying a few pros and/or cons about an allotment, with some comments on use of language and some quotation as evidence;
4–5 marks for a clear understanding of how language shows different pros and cons of an allotment, with quotations as evidence;
6 marks for a full analysis of how language shows different pros and cons of an allotment, well-supported by quotations.

6. **1 mark** for a simple awareness of pros and/or cons of an allotment;
2–3 marks for identifying a few pros and/or cons about an allotment, with some comments on use of structure and some quotation as evidence;
4–5 marks for a clear understanding of how structure shows different pros and cons of an allotment, with quotations as evidence;
6 marks for a full analysis of how structure shows different pros and cons of an allotment, well-supported by quotations.

Text C

7. **a.** Any suitable phrase, e.g. 'boisterously', 'swinging', 'the joy of wielding', 'waving the bottle around like a loaded cannon', 'enormous fun', 'what's not to like?'
   b. Explain how one or more specific words or techniques show how he makes ketchup sound fun. e.g. The simile 'like a loaded cannon' suggests the ketchup was exciting and linked to childhood games of being a soldier.

8. **1 mark** for a simple awareness of a criticism of the ketchup;
2–3 marks for identifying a few criticisms of the ketchup, with some comments on use of language and some quotation as evidence;
4–5 marks for a clear understanding of how language is used to criticise the ketchup, with quotations as evidence;
6 marks for a full analysis of how language is used to show criticism of the ketchup, well-supported by quotations.

9. **1–3 marks** for a simple awareness of praise for ketchup;
4–6 marks for identifying a few ways in which ketchup is good, with some comments on use of language and/or structure, and some quotation as evidence;
7–9 marks for a clear understanding of how language and structure are used to make ketchup sound good, with quotations as evidence;
10–12 marks for a full analysis of how language and structure are used to make ketchup sound good, well-supported by quotations.

Section 3
Texts A, B, and C
1–3 marks for a simple awareness of where the text is interesting/engaging/entertaining;
4–6 marks for identifying a few ways language and/or structure are used to make the text interesting/engaging/ entertaining, with some quotation as evidence;
7–9 marks for a clear understanding of how language and structure are used to make the text interesting/engaging/ entertaining, with quotation as evidence;
10–12 marks for a full analysis of how language and structure are used to make the text interesting/engaging/entertaining, well-supported by quotations.

Section 4
1. **1 mark** for a simple awareness of the two writers' lives;
2–3 marks for identifying a few similarities and/or differences between the two writers' lives, with some quotation as evidence;
4–5 marks for a clear understanding of similarities and differences between the two writers' lives, with quotation as evidence;
6 marks for a full understanding of similarities and differences between the two writers' lives, well-supported by quotations.

2. **1 mark** for a simple awareness of the children's behaviour;
2–3 marks for identifying a few similarities and/or differences between the children's behaviour, with some quotation as evidence;
4–5 marks for a clear understanding of similarities and differences between the children's behaviour, with quotation as evidence;
6 marks for a full understanding of similarities and differences between the children's behaviour, well-supported by quotations.

Section 5

1. **1–4 marks** for a simple awareness of the writers' enjoyment of food, with a few references to both texts;
5–8 marks for identifying several points about enjoyment of food and trying to compare, as well as some comment on use of language and/or structure, supported by some quotation;
9–12 marks for a clear understanding and comparison of how the writers show their enjoyment of food, with quotations as evidence;
13–16 marks for a full analysis and comparison, well-supported by quotations, of how the writers show their enjoyment of food.

2. **1–4 marks** for a simple awareness of the writers' love of nature and being outdoors, with a few references to both texts;
5–8 marks for identifying several points about loving nature and being outdoors, and trying to compare, as well as some comment on use of language and/or structure, supported by some quotation;
9–12 marks for a clear understanding and comparison of how the writers show their love of nature and being outdoors, with quotations as evidence;
13–16 marks for a full analysis and comparison, well-supported by quotations, of how the writers show their love of nature and being outdoors.

Day 2

pages 18–19
Ideas and Themes
QUICK TEST
1. **a.** Vera Claythorne
   b. Hot
   c. Holiday job as a secretary

EXAM PRACTICE
1. She is tired; she is pleased to have got a summer job; she has secretarial skills; she is a games teacher; she would like to work in a better school; she has been involved in a coroner's inquest; she has mixed feelings about the sea.
[1 mark for each, up to a maximum of 4]

2. She is travelling by train; she is in a third-class carriage; there are five other people in the carriage; it is hot; she caught the train at 12.40; she is travelling from Paddington (London) to Oakbridge (Devon); her journey has been paid for by her employers; she will be met at the station.
[1 mark for each, up to a maximum of 4]

3. 'there had been nothing else in the papers lately'; 'all sorts of hints and interesting rumours'; 'was said to be absolutely the last word in luxury'. **[1 mark for each quotation, up to a maximum of 2]**

4. **1 mark** for identifying that Vera would like a better teaching job but then feels grateful just for having a job;
1 mark for including one or two supporting quotations.

5. **1 mark** for identifying that she is looking forward to going to the coast (she expects it to be cooler/fresher) but then (when she thinks about the inquest) she wishes she wasn't going near the sea;
1 mark for including one or two supporting quotations.

pages 20–21
Language and Structure: Characters and Feelings
QUICK TEST
1. Appearance, behaviour, speech, feelings and attitudes
2. To prove where you got your idea from and to give you words/phrases to analyse
3. 'Flung' suggests she is excited or in a rush

EXAM PRACTICE
1. **1–2 marks** for simple awareness of what Tamara is like;
3–4 marks for identifying a few things about Tamara, with some comments on use of language and/or structure, and some quotation as evidence;
5–6 marks for a clear understanding of how language and structure are used to present the character of Tamara, with quotations as evidence;
7–8 marks for a full analysis of how language and structure are used to present the character of Tamara, well-supported by quotations.

2. **1–2 marks** for simple awareness of Tamara's feelings about clothes;
3–4 marks for identifying one or two things about Tamara's attitude to clothes, with some comments on use of language and/or structure, and some quotation as evidence;
5–6 marks for a clear understanding of Tamara's attitude to clothes, with quotations as evidence;
7–8 marks for a full analysis of how language and structure are used to show Tamara's attitude to clothes, well-supported by quotations.

pages 22–23
Language and Structure: Setting and Mood

QUICK TEST

1. The main feelings in a piece of writing
2. Any four suitable synonyms, e.g. pleased, cheerful, overjoyed, ecstatic; quiet, relaxed, tranquil, serene; creepy, chilling, frightening, terrifying
3. Mental or emotional strain felt by the reader and/or a character

EXAM PRACTICE

1. **1–2 marks** for simple awareness of what the room is like; **3–4 marks** for identifying a few things about the room, with some comments on use of language and/or structure, and some quotation as evidence; **5–6 marks** for a clear understanding of how language and structure are used to describe the room, with quotations as evidence; **7–8 marks** for a full analysis of how language and structure are used to describe the room, well-supported by quotations.
2. **1–3 marks** for simple awareness of what is sinister; **4–6 marks** for identifying one or two things that create a sinister atmosphere, with some comments on use of language and/or structure, and some quotation as evidence; **7–9 marks** for a clear understanding of how the writer creates a sinister atmosphere, with quotations as evidence; **10–12 marks** for a full analysis of how language and structure are used to create a sinister atmosphere, well-supported by quotations.

pages 24–25
Narrative Structure

QUICK TEST

1. First person can emphasise thought and emotion, and can heighten suspense as the narrator isn't all-knowing, whereas third person offers more breadth of character, settings, events, etc.
2. Makes you read on for a resolution
3. Start, middle, and end

EXAM PRACTICE

1. **1–2 marks** for a simple awareness of what is interesting about the extract; **3–4 marks** for using some of the bullet point prompts to identify things that are interesting about the extract, with some comments on use of structure, and some quotation as evidence; **5–6 marks** for a clear understanding of how the extract has been structured to interest the reader, responding to most or all of the bullet point prompts and using quotations as evidence; **7–8 marks** for a full analysis, responding to all bullet point prompts, of how the extract has been structured to interest the reader, well-supported by quotations.

pages 26–27
Engaging the Reader

QUICK TEST

1. Language, sentence structure and narrative structure
2. It may help you to understand why ideas are being organised in a certain way (e.g. to introduce at the start, to develop in the middle, to resolve or create a cliffhanger at the end).
3. The short sentence makes the information stand out, which grabs the reader's attention. The reader is also directly involved through the use of a question. The use of past tense in 'were' is unusual and should make the reader wonder why they no longer exist or have the family name.

EXAM PRACTICE

1. **1–4 marks** for a simple awareness of what is engaging about the extract; **5–8 marks** for identifying a few things that are engaging about the extract, with some comments on use of language, and/or sentence structure, and/or narrative structure, and some quotation as evidence; **9–12 marks** for a clear understanding of how language and sentence structure and/or narrative structure are used to make the extract an engaging opening, with quotations as evidence; **13–16 marks** for a full analysis of how language, sentence structure, and narrative structure have been used to make the extract an engaging opening, well-supported by quotations.

pages 28–29
Debating and Comparing

QUICK TEST

1. Structure a simple debate, making points that agree and disagree with the given statement about the text.
2. 'This is particularly successful…', 'The most effective way…', 'The writer makes good use of…', etc.

3. Come up with clear points of comparison about the two texts.

EXAM PRACTICE

1. **1–4 marks** for a simple awareness of how the text links to the statement;
   5–8 marks for identifying a few links between the statement and the text, with some comments on use of language and/or structure, and some quotation as evidence;
   9–12 marks for a clear understanding of how language and structure in the text link to both sides of the given statement, with quotations as evidence and some evaluative comment;
   13–16 marks for a full analysis and evaluation of how language and structure in the text link to both sides of the given statement, well-supported by quotations.
2. **1–4 marks** for a simple awareness of how the text links to the statement;
   5–8 marks for identifying a few links between the statement and the text, with some comments on use of language and/or structure, and some quotation as evidence;
   9–12 marks for a clear understanding of how language and structure in the text link to both sides of the given statement, with quotations as evidence and some evaluative comment;
   13–16 marks for a full analysis and evaluation of how language and structure in the text link to both sides of the given statement, well-supported by quotations.
3. **1–4 marks** for a simple awareness of how the statement links to one or both texts;
   5–8 marks for identifying one or two ways each text links to the statement, with some comparison and comments on use of language and/or structure, and some quotation as evidence;
   9–12 marks for identifying some basic comparisons of how the texts link to the statement, some consideration of both sides of the statement, with comments on use of language and/or structure, and quotations as evidence;
   13–16 marks for a clear understanding and comparison of how the texts link to the statement, looking at both sides of the statement, with some analysis and evaluation of language and/or structure as well as quotations as evidence;
   17–20 marks for a full analysis, structured comparison, and some evaluation of how language and structure in the texts link to both sides of the statement, well-supported by quotations;
   21–24 marks for a structured comparison offering a full and subtle analysis and evaluation of how language and structure link to both sides of the statement, well-supported by quotations.

With this type of question, make sure you engage with the statement that you have been given. You can agree or disagree with it but always try to see the alternative view as well. Remember that, to get the top marks, you need to be actively evaluating the effectiveness of the writer's choices of language and structure, but do not fall into the trap of suggesting how you could write it differently!

pages 30–31
Fiction Exam Practice
Ideas and Themes

1. For example: pinched face, waxy skin, sunken eyes, wore glasses, tall and slim, stooped, seemed in a rush, etc. **[1 mark for each, up to a maximum of 4]**
2. For example: 'at approximately 6:15am', 'so early', 'dawn', etc. **[1 mark for each, up to a maximum of 2]**
3. **1 mark** for identifying that at first the man just seems strange or looks unusual but that the gatekeeper then realises he plans to commit suicide;
   1 mark for including one or two supporting quotations.

Language and Structure: Characters and Feelings

1. **1–2 marks** for a simple awareness of what the man is like;
   3–4 marks for identifying a few things about the man, with some comments on use of language and/or structure, and some quotation as evidence;
   5–6 marks for a clear understanding of how language and structure are used to show what the man is like, with quotations as evidence;
   7–8 marks for a full analysis of how language and structure are used to present the man, well-supported by quotations.

Language and Structure: Setting and Mood

1. **1–2 marks** for a simple awareness of what the Niagara Falls are like;
   3–4 marks for identifying a few things about the Falls, with some comments on use of language and/or structure, and some quotation as evidence;
   5–6 marks for a clear understanding of how language and structure are used to describe the Falls, with quotations as evidence;
   7–8 marks for a full analysis of how language and structure are used to describe the Falls, well-supported by quotations.
2. **1–3 marks** for a simple awareness of where there is tension in the text;
   4–6 marks for identifying a few points where tension is created, with some comments on use of language and/or structure, and some quotation as evidence;
   7–9 marks for a clear understanding of how tension is created through language and structure, with some sense of its build-up, and quotations as evidence;
   10–12 marks for a full analysis of how language and structure are used to build tension, well-supported by quotations.

Narrative Structure

1. **1–2 marks** for a simple awareness of what is interesting about the extract;

   3–4 marks for identifying a few things that are interesting about the extract, with some comments on use of structure, and some quotation as evidence;

   5–6 marks for a clear understanding of how the extract has been structured to interest the reader, using quotations as evidence;

   7–8 marks for a full analysis of how the extract has been structured to interest the reader, well-supported by quotations.

Engaging the Reader

1. **1–4 marks** for a simple awareness of what is engaging about the extract;

   5–8 marks for identifying a few things that are engaging about the extract, with some comments on use of language, and/or sentence structure, and/or narrative structure, and some quotation as evidence;

   9–12 marks for a clear understanding of how language and sentence structure and/or narrative structure are used to make the extract an engaging opening, with quotations as evidence;

   13–16 marks for a full analysis of how language, sentence structure, and narrative structure have been used to make the extract an engaging opening, well-supported by quotations.

Debating and Comparing

1. **1–4 marks** for a simple awareness of how the text links to the statement;

   5–8 marks for identifying a few links between the statement and the text, with some comments on use of language and/or structure, and some quotation as evidence;

   9–12 marks for a clear understanding of how language and structure in the text link to both sides of the given statement, with quotations as evidence and some evaluative comment;

   13–16 marks for a full analysis and evaluation of how language and structure in the text link to both sides of the given statement, well-supported by quotations.

Day 3

pages 32–33
Planning Your Writing
QUICK TEST
1. Purpose, Audience, Form
2. Chronologically or thematically.
3. Spelling, punctuation, and grammar; conveying and developing ideas effectively

EXAM PRACTICE
1. Ideas in your plan might include: your hobby/interest; what it entails; when you do it; what got you into it; what you enjoy about it.
2. Ideas in your plan might include: a clear response to the statement (agree, disagree, or a combination of both); the different problems we are causing the world due to not recycling enough; different ways in which recycling is easy.

pages 34–35
Spelling
QUICK TEST
1. **a.** author
   b. playwright
   c. simile
   d. atmosphere
   e. sentence
   f. character
   g. Shakespeare

PRACTICE
1. fourty/forty; brake/break; minites/minutes; enjoyeble/enjoyable; readding/reading; you're/your mum; stressfull/stressful; strugling/struggling; compleat/complete; techneques/techniques; no/know are; usefull/useful; too/to read; there/their notes; copie/copy; thier/their; actully/actually; knew/new one; acheive/achieve; successfull/successful; sugested/suggested; resentting/resenting; addishun/addition; they're/there is; appropriatly/appropriately; two/too much; allways/always; to/too little; freinds/friends; swiming/swimming

pages 36–37
Grammar and Punctuation
QUICK TEST
1. **a.** Jack's first day, cleaning at Everton Football Club, was going well.
   b. Although she loved them, Shirley disliked cleaning her dogs' kennels.
   c. In Bristol's city centre, Dave was walking to Waterstones to buy JK Rowling's latest book.

PRACTICE
1. The figure began to follow Holly towards the house, its black cloak billowing in the breeze.
   The figure, its black cloak billowing in the breeze, began to follow Holly towards the house.
   Moving as softly as a whisper, the advancing figure seemed to merge with the darkness of the night.
   The advancing figure, moving as softly as a whisper, seemed to merge with the darkness of the night.

2. Holly kept running. She <u>didn't</u> know where she was anymore but she knew there was no time to stop and look around. As <u>Holly's</u> feet pounded the pavement, she felt her heart thumping through her ribcage. Buildings, hedges, signposts, and parked cars all passed in a blur of panic and adrenalin. <u>She</u> had to keep going in case they were still behind her. Suddenly, <u>its</u> familiar red doorway shining in the moonlight, she recognised <u>Darren's</u> house. It was hard to believe she had run so far. Daring to glance behind her, Holly saw an empty street. She was alone but was she safe? As she headed for the red door, a dark figure stepped out from the shadows.

> *Using correct punctuation and grammar may not come naturally to you. Often this is because, although you know the rules, you spend most of your time (apart from in your English lessons) not worrying about your technical accuracy. To remedy this, you should consciously make the effort to always write correctly. At first, this will slow you down but, gradually, it will become second-nature and you won't be making lots of mistakes.*

pages 38–39
Writing to Describe
QUICK TEST
1. Sight, sound, smell, touch, taste
2. Before, after, or in the middle
3. Short sentence
4. List

EXAM PRACTICE
1–3. Content and Organisation

1–4 marks (approximately Level 1):
Basic response; purpose, audience, and form not fully established; limited use of structural and organisational features.

10–14 marks (approximately Level 4–5):
Selects ideas and devices to suit purpose, audience, and form; appropriate tone, style, and register; ideas are developed and connected; clearly structured, using paragraphs and other organisational features.

20–24 marks (approximately Level 8–9):
Full understanding of purpose, audience, and form is shown through the way writing is shaped to achieve specific effects; tone, style, and register are sophisticated and sustained; ideas are complex and cohesive; a range of structural and organisational features successfully heighten the effectiveness of the writing.

Technical Accuracy

1–3 marks (approximately Level 1):
Basic vocabulary with regular spelling errors; basic punctuation; undeveloped, often repetitive sentence structures.

7–9 marks (approximately Level 4–5):
Varied vocabulary with correct spelling of most words, including some with irregular patterns; accurate and varied punctuation; some range of sentence structures used for effect.

13–16 marks (approximately Level 8–9):
Extensive vocabulary which is used for effect; spelling errors are rare; varied and accurate punctuation is used to emphasise, or increase precision of, ideas; a full range of sentence structures successfully achieves specific effects.

> *Writing to describe should be easy because you have been doing it since you were in primary school. However, students often fall into the trap of getting carried away with their own imagination. This means that their writing lacks technical accuracy and does not contain much actual description (instead, being full of events or dialogue). Take your time! Consciously use language and structure to create vivid ideas and images in your reader's mind. Show off all your different descriptive skills.*

pages 40–41
Writing From a Stimulus
QUICK TEST
1. Inspire
2. Who, what, where, when, why, how?
3. Language, sentence structure, and narrative structure

EXAM PRACTICE
1–4. See Exam Practice mark scheme for pages 38–39.

pages 42–43
Writing to Inform and Explain
QUICK TEST
1. Connectives of time/place
2. Progression, and cause and effect
3. Because you are providing the reader with information about a topic

EXAM PRACTICE
1–3. See Exam Practice mark scheme for pages 38–39.

pages 44–45
Writing to Argue and Persuade
QUICK TEST
1. Trying to get the reader to think or do something
2. Facts, Opinions, Rhetorical questions, Emotion and Empathy; Statistics, Triplets, Repetition, You
3. Sequence, progression, contrast, and cause and effect

EXAM PRACTICE
1–3. See Exam Practice mark scheme for pages 38–39.

pages 46–47
Writing to Advise and Instruct
QUICK TEST
1. Writing to advise is friendly and more informal; writing to instruct is more formal and impersonal
2. Verbs that show necessity, possibility and ability
3. Sequence

EXAM PRACTICE
1–3. See Exam Practice mark scheme for pages 38–39.

Day 4

pages 48–49
Poetic Techniques
QUICK TEST
1. e
2. b
3. d
4. a
5. c

PRACTICE
1. The cold simile suggests the man doesn't feel anything, emotionally, for the speaker.
2. The metaphor suggests the photograph reminds him of lots of different things about his mother and that, as a result, he cannot control his grief.
3. The sibilance links to the hiss of the snake as well as highlighting, through alliteration, its movements.
4. The plosives and onomatopoeia emphasise how unbearably loud he finds his neighbours.
5. The speaker seems haunted and tempted by the house, almost scared of it, as if it has power over him.

pages 50–51
Structural Techniques
QUICK TEST
1. c
2. d
3. a
4. b

PRACTICE
1. It emphasises all the work his mother does by piling up verbs one after the other.
2. They suggest the anger caused by being upset by someone.
3. It emphasises how difficult it is to discover the person's true feelings, as well as exaggerating the emotion in the lines.
4. The speaker cannot work out which emotion the person feels. It also suggests the two can be closely linked.

5. The speaker seems desperate for some reassurance that they are loved by the person who is going away.

pages 52–53
Form
QUICK TEST
1. Metre
2. Love
3. A poem where a character speaks to an audience (one or more people) but the audience does not actually appear or reply.

PRACTICE
1. a. Sonnet
   b. The poem is written in iambic pentameter; it has three quatrains, rhyming *abab*, and ends with a rhyming couplet.
   c. Rhyming couplet
   d. They explain the poem: he has realised what she is really like; he feels that love is like an illness because he has fallen in love with someone who treats him badly.
   e. The short lines with their rigid metre and rhyme scheme could mirror how he feels trapped inside his unhealthy relationship.

pages 54–55
Poetry Anthology: Themes
QUICK TEST
1. For example, if you are studying Love and Relationships the sub-themes might include: romantic love, family relationships, sexual desire, unrequited love, happy/unhappy relationships.
2. For example, if you are studying Love and Relationships, which of your poems link to romantic love, which link to sexual desire, etc?
3. Language, structure and form

EXAM PRACTICE
1. **1–2 marks** (approximately Level 1):
   Basic, sometimes unfocussed response; one or two quotations or references to the poem.

   6–10 marks (approximately Level 4–5):
   A clear, sustained response, focussed on the question, showing a good understanding of ideas and viewpoints; relevant quotations; clear explanations of different ways in which language, structure, and/or form have been used to convey meaning; some use of terminology.

   14–18 marks (approximately Level 8–9):
   A detailed, perceptive, and focussed response, providing a full exploration of ideas and viewpoints; well-chosen, precise quotations; a range of terminology used to analyse

the different methods of language, structure, and form by which the poet conveys meaning.

If you do not yet feel confident with the poems in your anthology, spend lots of time re-reading them until they feel familiar. You should not be scared by the idea of poetry! Think of the poems as little stories or powerful descriptions of experiences.

pages 56–57
Poetry Anthology: Comparison
QUICK TEST
1. Quotations
2. Analyse it
3. Connectives of comparison

EXAM PRACTICE
1. **1–4 marks** (approximately Level 1):
   Basic, sometimes unfocussed response; some awareness of similarities and/or differences; one or two quotations or references to the poems.
   13–20 marks (approximately Level 4–5):
   A clear, sustained comparison, focussed on the question, with specific links showing a good understanding of ideas and viewpoints; relevant quotations; clear explanations of different ways in which language, structure, and/or form have been used to convey meaning; some use of terminology.
   29–36 marks (approximately Level 8–9):
   A detailed, perceptive, and focussed comparison, with a variety of links providing a full exploration of ideas and viewpoints; well-chosen, precise quotations; a range of terminology used to analyse the different methods of language, structure, and form by which the poets convey meaning.

Plan your ideas and remember to compare. Some students end up writing everything they know about one poem, followed by everything they know about the other poem! Keep focussed on the exam question and alternate your points between the two poems, using connectives of comparisons to clearly link your ideas.

pages 58–59
Analysing Unseen Poetry
QUICK TEST
1. Theme, Images, Form, Structure
2. Once you have some themes you can start analysing how images, form, and structure have been used to convey meaning.
3. Analyse its effect: how is it conveying meaning?

EXAM PRACTICE
1. See Exam Practice mark scheme for pages 54–55.
   Ideas might include:

Images: happy and peaceful metaphors, similes, verbs, and adjectives; images of brightness; symbolism using colours (gold = value; white = innocence); use of different senses, including onomatopoeia to help the reader imagine the scene. Form: the poem is a sonnet (traditional form for love poetry). Structure: anaphora/repetition of 'I love'; list of all the things he likes about summer; lack of punctuation (even at the end) to suggest the list is endless.

When you get an unseen text (whether it is poetry, fiction or non-fiction), try not to panic if there are bits that you do not understand. Students do this a lot, especially if the text is written before the 20th century. Instead, focus on what you do understand and the different features and techniques that you can explore.

pages 60–63
Comparing Unseen Poetry
QUICK TEST
1. Images (language), form, and structure
2. To highlight your comparisons
3. The first sentence is a clear point of comparison. The second sentence contains the quotation and the third sentence has the analysis. The fifth sentence begins with a connective and ends with a quotation. The final two sentences contain analysis.

EXAM PRACTICE
1–3. See Exam Practice mark scheme for pages 56–57.
   Ideas for *First Love* might include:
   Similes and metaphors to show the pain and awkwardness of love; use of repetition/anaphora to show how she affects his life; superlative adjective to show how much he loves her; use of negative verbs, adjectives, and adverbs to describe negative aspects of falling in love; use of hyperbole to suggest first love is over-the-top because it is so different to previous feelings; changes in tone (humour and sadness); repetition to emphasise blindness and foolishness of love; free verse and lack of punctuation suggests the confusion of first love as well as its limitless passion; lack of final full stop to emphasise the idea that the boy thinks the love will last forever.

   Ideas for *A Birthday* might include:
   Similes to show the effects of love; anaphora/repetition to focus on the heart (symbolising love); use of list to build up her happiness; verbs and adjectives to create a sense of celebration; repetition at the end of each stanza to emphasise the cause of her happiness; use of 'birthday' to suggest the effect of love upon her; each line of the octets (eight lines) contains eight syllables which might reflect the perfection she feels her life has achieved; the fact there are two of these octets could link to the idea of her and him.

Day 5

pages 64–65

Shakespeare: Character

QUICK TEST

1. **Julius Caesar**
   Metaphor and an adverb are used to present Brutus as an honourable man who will put his country before his life.

   Macbeth
   Metaphor is used to show what Lady Macbeth hopes she and her husband will achieve; metaphor and personification show how she plans to manipulate him (and how she sees this as one of her skills).

   Much Ado About Nothing
   Beatrice uses exclamations and simile to mock Benedick and suggest he is irritating and a bad influence on others.

   Romeo and Juliet
   Metaphor is used to show how Lord Capulet values Juliet as his only child; rhyme is used to emphasise that he wants Juliet to marry someone she loves.

   The Tempest
   Rhetorical question and the noun 'pains' are used to show how Ariel sees Prospero as a harsh controller.

   The Merchant of Venice
   Adjectives and repetition are used to show Bassanio's love for Portia.

   Twelfth Night
   Metaphor and simile are used to show how Duke Orsino feels like a victim of love.

2. Own answer.
3. Own answer.

EXAM PRACTICE

1. **1–4 marks** (approximately Level 1):
   Basic, sometimes unfocussed response; some awareness of character or theme; one or two quotations or references to the play.
   13–20 marks (approximately Level 4–5):
   A clear, sustained response, focussed on the question, with specific links showing a good understanding of character or theme; relevant quotations; clear explanations of different ways in which language, structure, and/or form have been used to convey meaning; some use of terminology.
   29–36 marks (approximately Level 8–9):
   A detailed, perceptive, and focussed response, with a variety of points providing a full exploration of character or theme; well-chosen, precise quotations; a range of terminology used to analyse the different methods of language, structure, and form by which Shakespeare conveys meaning.

pages 66–67

Shakespeare: Character Development

QUICK TEST

1. **Julius Caesar**
   The euphemism for murder and the irony of 'friends' shows his betrayal of Caesar. The repetition of 'our' and the imperative 'stoop' suggests he wants to become leader.

   Macbeth
   'Blood' symbolises the guilt she now feels; the adjective 'little' and the three exclamations show how her madness has weakened her.

   Much Ado About Nothing
   Personification and metaphor show Beatrice deciding to think differently about Benedick and love.

   Romeo and Juliet
   Threats, insults, and exclamation show Lord Capulet's anger with his daughter because she won't follow his orders.

   The Tempest
   Questions, metaphor and the respectful word 'master' show Ariel's willingness to do what Prospero wants.

   The Merchant of Venice
   Metaphor is used to emphasise Bassanio's love for Portia.

   Twelfth Night
   Adjectives and metaphor are used to emphasise how Duke Orsino feels Olivia treats him badly by not returning his love.

2. Own answer.
3. Own answer.

EXAM PRACTICE

1. See Exam Practice mark scheme for pages 64–65.

pages 68–69

Shakespeare: Themes and Context

QUICK TEST

1. For example:
   Julius Caesar
   Persuasion, leadership, compromise, public vs private, fate.

   Macbeth
   Power, leadership vs tyranny, persuasion, violence, the supernatural.

   Much Ado About Nothing
   Deception and disguise, honour and shame, masculinity and femininity, love and marriage, the battle of the sexes.

   Romeo and Juliet
   Love, violence, fate and coincidence, family, vengeance.

The Tempest

Leadership, love, good and evil, magic and reality, betrayal and vengeance.

The Merchant of Venice

Love, mercy, hatred, self-interest and greed, deception.

Twelfth Night

Love, ambition, gender roles, suffering, class.

2. For example:

Julius Caesar

The empire of ancient Rome mirroring Elizabethan England; divisions between the military leaders, the citizens, and the plebeians; belief in omens and portents.

Macbeth

James I's Scottish lineage, interest in witches, and issues of divine right; historical, feudal setting when the monarchy was more unstable; traditional expectations of gender.

Much Ado About Nothing

Traditional expectations of women and social behaviour; comic traditions.

Romeo and Juliet

Traditional expectations of women, parents, social behaviour and marriage.

The Tempest

English colonialism; Christian values of love and forgiveness.

The Merchant of Venice

Christianity and Judaism; Elizabethan anti-Semitism; traditional expectations of women.

Twelfth Night

Traditional expectation of gender and sexuality; Elizabethan theatre with all roles being played by men; comic traditions.

3. *Julius Caesar*

The ignoring of the Soothsayer goes against tradition and shows Caesar's arrogance, as well as introducing the theme of fate and omens.

Macbeth

Macbeth's words link to his breaching of the Divine Right of Kings; Lady Macbeth seems to have less conscience than her husband.

Much Ado About Nothing

These lines link to traditional expectations of a woman's virtue and the idea of sex as sinful.

Romeo and Juliet

Lord Capulet presents his traditional role as head of the household; the theme of love is also explored through his belief that he can make Juliet's choice for her.

The Tempest

These lines explore Christian attitudes to forgiveness as well as the theme of mind and reason over body and instinct.

The Merchant of Venice

As well as Shylock's traditional expectations of Jessica as his daughter and as a woman, we can see the clash between Judaism and Christianity.

Twelfth Night

As well as exploring ideas about gender, humour is emphasised through the traditional Shakespearean staging where all roles were played by men.

EXAM PRACTICE

1. See Exam Practice mark scheme for page 64–65.

Avoid summarising all the points of context that you know about your play in the introduction to your exam response. Instead, try to link them to your analysis at different points in your essay. This will show that you understand how the context can affect our interpretation of the play, rather than simply what the context is.

pages 70–71

Shakespeare: Learning Quotations

QUICK TEST

1–4. Complete each task until you can remember the whole quote.

PRACTICE

1. You might include:

Julius Caesar

Verbs and abstract nouns are used to show how important reputation is to Brutus.

Macbeth

Metaphor and exclamations show Macbeth's conscience tormenting him.

Much Ado About Nothing

Insults, exclamation, and rhetorical questions portray the battle of the sexes between Beatrice and Benedick in a humorous way.

Romeo and Juliet

Personification, an adjective, a rhetorical question, and short sentence emphasise Romeo's love at first sight for Juliet.

The Tempest

Adjectives, insults, and an imperative suggest how bad Caliban is whilst also presenting Prospero's power.

The Merchant of Venice

List, pause, and exclamation are used to emphasise Portia's love for Bassanio.

Twelfth Night
Rhyme, exclamation, and the aside are used to create humour in Viola's situation.

pages 72–73
Shakespeare: Working With and Beyond an Extract
QUICK TEST
1. She is devious; she is linked to the devil.
2. Simile, metaphor, plosives, sibilance, traditional imagery, biblical imagery, rhetorical question, irony, soliloquy, superlative adjective
3. Traditional imagery (the time Shakespeare was writing), expectations of women (different audience response), religion and the king (the setting of the play).

EXAM PRACTICE
1. See Exam Practice mark scheme for pages 64–65.

> It can seem much easier just to write about the extract that you are given. Some students panic in the exam and forget to also write about the rest of the play. Instead, remember to answer both parts of the question. If you go blank and cannot think of any quotations, do not stop writing; just make specific references to scenes and things that characters do or say.

Day 6
pages 74–75
19th Century Prose: Character
QUICK TEST
1. **The Strange Case of Dr Jekyll and Mr Hyde**
   Nouns and a list of adjectives are used to present Dr Jekyll as a good person.

   A Christmas Carol
   Similes and adjectives are used to present Scrooge as private, unfriendly, and emotionally cold.

   Great Expectations
   A list of verbs show the things Magwitch has been through, suggesting his strength and determination as well as getting some sympathy from the reader.

   Jane Eyre
   A list of verbs, repetition of 'always', and rhetorical questions show Jane's unhappiness and the unfairness of her situation.

Frankenstein
Metaphors and nouns show Frankenstein's intellectual curiosity and his excitement at scientific discovery.

Pride and Prejudice
The adjectives and the pattern of three emphasise Mrs Bennet's poor qualities.

The Sign of Four
Adjectives are used to show Sherlock's drug abuse.

War of the Worlds
Metaphor and a list are used to show the narrator's excitement at the idea of Martians.

Silas Marner
Contrast and biblical language are used to show Marner's lack of faith in the world.

2. Own answer.
3. Own answer.

EXAM PRACTICE
1. **1–4 marks** (approximately Level 1):
   Basic, sometimes unfocussed response; some awareness of character or theme; one or two quotations or references to the novel.

   13–20 marks (approximately Level 4–5):
   A clear, sustained response, focussed on the question, with specific links showing a good understanding of character or theme; relevant quotations; clear explanations of different ways in which language, structure, and/or form have been used to convey meaning; some use of terminology.

   29–36 marks (approximately Level 8–9):
   A detailed, perceptive, and focussed response, with a variety of points providing a full exploration of character or theme; well-chosen, precise quotations; a range of terminology used to analyse the different methods of language, structure, and form by which the novelist conveys meaning.

pages 76–77
19th Century Prose: Character Development
QUICK TEST
1. **The Strange Case of Dr Jekyll and Mr Hyde**
   Negative language is used to show Mr Hyde as Dr Jekyll's dark side; contrasting, positive language is used to show Jekyll's fascination with this side of his character.

   A Christmas Carol
   The list of virtuous actions shows the change in Scrooge.

   Great Expectations
   The verbs and repetition show Magwitch's gratitude to Pip.

   Jane Eyre
   Metaphor is used to show Jane's feelings that her fortunes are changing.

Frankenstein

Adjectives and abstract nouns are used to show Frankenstein's hatred for the product of his experiments.

Pride and Prejudice

Adjectives are used to highlight Mrs Bennet's poor qualities and the effect they have on her daughters.

The Sign of Four

The short sentence, exclamations, and question show how Holmes is able to surprise and outwit even his closest friends.

War of the Worlds

Short sentences, alliterations, and powerful verbs are used to show the narrator's desperate act of murder.

Silas Marner

Metaphor and repetition are used to show Marner's discovery of faith in the world.

2. Own answer.
3. Own answer.

EXAM PRACTICE

1. See Exam Practice mark scheme for pages 74–75.

pages 78–79
19th Century Prose: Themes
QUICK TEST

1. For example:

   The Strange Case of Dr Jekyll and Mr Hyde

   Good vs evil, science, deception, appearance, morality, instinct.

   A Christmas Carol

   Guilt, compassion, forgiveness, poverty, family, time, transformation.

   Great Expectations

   Family, ambition, class, money, deception, love, betrayal, compassion.

   Jane Eyre

   Love, marriage, morality, education, social class, the supernatural.

   Frankenstein

   Science vs nature, religion, compassion, isolation, companionship, violence, vengeance.

   Pride and Prejudice

   Pride, prejudice, love and marriage, social class, family, deception, principles.

   The Sign of Four

   Good and evil, crime, intelligence, disguise and deception, empire and fear of foreignness.

War of the Worlds

Science and technology, aliens, war and violence, empire and invasion, fear, isolation, the breakdown of civilisation.

Silas Marner

Change and (mis)fortune, wealth and greed, religion, isolation.

2. Own answer.

3. *The Strange Case of Dr Jekyll and Mr Hyde*

   The verb 'exposed' shows that Jekyll is keen to maintain the image of a gentleman.

   A Christmas Carol

   The comparative adjective and the simile contrast with the verb 'kept' to show Scrooge's selfishness.

   Great Expectations

   Adjectives and metaphor suggest that people should stay faithful to their origins.

   Jane Eyre

   The contrast of pronouns (you; us/our) and the use of words linked to poverty show Jane's low position in the household.

   Frankenstein

   Verbs show the Creature's wish, but inability, to be part of society.

   Pride and Prejudice

   The use of exclamations and the repetition of 'single' show Mrs Bennet's desperation to marry her daughters to rich men.

   The Sign of Four

   Personification and adjectives make danger sound scary; contrasting verbs show Sherlock's relaxed attitude to danger.

   War of the Worlds

   Short sentence, metaphors, and adjectives convey the fear of the narrator and those around him.

   Silas Marner

   Metaphor and verbs show the limits of Marner's life.

EXAM PRACTICE

1. See Exam Practice mark scheme for pages 74–75.

pages 80–81
19th Century Prose: Context
QUICK TEST

1. For example:

   The Strange Case of Dr Jekyll and Mr Hyde

   Victorian values, class, social expectations, social problems, science.

A Christmas Carol
Victorian values, social problems, religion.

Great Expectations
Victorian values, class, social expectations, gender.

Jane Eyre
Victorian values, class, social expectations, gender, religion.

Frankenstein
Religion, science.

Pride and Prejudice
Class, social expectations, gender.

The Sign of Four
Victorian values, social expectations, social problems, empire.

War of the Worlds
Victorian values, science, empire.

Silas Marner
Industrialisation, social problems, religion, gender.

2. Own answer.
3. Own answer.

EXAM PRACTICE
1. See Exam Practice mark scheme for pages 74–75.

> If you are struggling with the idea of context and understanding what the 19th century was like, look out for adaptations of your novel or similar novels from the same period. Providers like Netflix, YouTube, and iPlayer can be great sources of Victorian-based television programmes and films. Pay attention to how people look and behave, their different living conditions, and contrasts between different social groups. This is also a more relaxing way of doing some revision!

pages 82–83
19th Century Prose: Working With and Beyond an Extract
QUICK TEST
1. She is mentally damaged; she is disturbing and manipulative
2. Adjective, contrast, metaphor, exclamation, foreshadowing, abstract nouns, sibilance, double meaning, first person narrative voice
3. 19th century Christian morality

EXAM PRACTICE
1. See Exam Practice mark scheme for pages 74–75.

Day 7
pages 84–85
20th Century Texts: Character
QUICK TEST
1. Personal pronouns, repetition, adjectives, dramatic irony
2. Use of imperatives to show dominant character; reference to the Titanic to reinforce dramatic irony
3. Birling's boastful adjectives can be interpreted differently in light of his job; the time in which the play is set, compared to when it was written, allows dramatic irony to be created.

EXAM PRACTICE
1. **1–4 marks** (approximately Level 1):
   Basic, sometimes unfocussed response; some awareness of character or theme; one or two quotations or references to the modern text.
   13–20 marks (approximately Level 4–5):
   A clear, sustained response, focussed on the question, with specific links showing a good understanding of character or theme; relevant quotations; clear explanations of different ways in which language, structure, and/or form have been used to convey meaning; some use of terminology.
   29–36 marks (approximately Level 8–9):
   A detailed, perceptive, and focussed response, with a variety of points providing a full exploration of character or theme; well-chosen, precise quotations; a range of terminology used to analyse the different methods of language, structure, and form by which the writer conveys meaning.

pages 86–87
20th Century Texts: Character Development
QUICK TEST
1–3. Own answers.

EXAM PRACTICE
1. See Exam Practice mark scheme for pages 84–85.

> When you are writing about how a character changes, keep focussed on how this is shown by the writer. Do not just point out what a character does or feels differently, try to analyse how the writer is using different language or sentence structures to convey change.

Answers

pages 88–89
20th Century Texts: Relationships and Importance

QUICK TEST

1–3. Own answers.

EXAM PRACTICE

1–2. See Exam Practice mark scheme for pages 84–85.

> *If you are writing about the importance or significance of a character, remember to analyse. Some students just write about why the character plays a key role in the text, rather than explaining how this is shown through the writer's choices of language and structure.*

pages 90–91
20th Century Texts: Themes

QUICK TEST

1–3. Own answers.

EXAM PRACTICE

1. See Exam Practice mark scheme for pages 84–85.

> *Remember to think about whether you have been studying a play or prose. As well as analysing how language and structure are used to explore a theme, try to comment on the effects of form (such as stage directions or monologues in a play, or first-person narrative or cliffhangers in prose).*

Glossary

Adjective	a describing word
Adverb	a word that describes a verb
Alliteration	a series of words beginning with the same sound
Anaphora	when words are repeated in a structured way (e.g. at the start of each new paragraph)
Audience	the people being addressed by a writer or speaker
Balanced argument	presenting both sides of an issue
Chronological	organising things in the order in which they happened
Complex sentence	a sentence comprising of a main clause and a subordinate clause
Compound sentence	a sentence combining two main clauses, joined by a conjunction
Conclusion	an end summary, making any necessary judgements about your topic
Conditional	something that is dependent on something else happening
Conjunction	a joining word, such as 'and', 'but', 'if'
Connective	a word or phrase that links ideas, such as 'however', 'in contrast'
Descriptive	creating images to help a reader imagine something
Develop	to clarify an idea, build upon it, or take it in a new direction
Effect	the result or consequence of something
Emotive language	words or phrases that convey or create powerful feelings
Empathy	sympathising with someone else's emotions
Emphasis	stressing, or attaching importance to, something
Euphemism	replacing a harsh, blunt phrase with something that sounds nicer
Exclamation	something exclaimed, as if in shock
Extended metaphor	a series of similar metaphors combining to create one image
Fact	something that can be proven
Form	the kind of text a piece of writing is for, e.g. a leaflet or newspaper
Formal	following rules or convention, not relaxed
Future tense	describing events that will happen
Imagery	words and phrases that build up pictures in the reader's mind
Imperative	an order
Irony	getting across your point whilst appearing to state the opposite
List	a series of words, items or small ideas
Main clause	the main part of a sentence (it should make sense on its own)
Metaphor	a descriptive comparison written as if it is true (rather than using 'like' or 'as')
Modal verb	a verb that shows the mood or state of another verb
Onomatopoeia	the use of words that sound like the sound they describe, e.g. 'pop'
Opinions	something that is thought or felt
Order	telling someone what to do
Pace	the speed of a piece of writing or speech
Paragraph	a section of writing
Past tense	describing events that have happened

Pause	a break in speech or writing
Personification	describing an object or abstract concept as if it has human qualities
Plan	the detailed method by which something will be done
Plosives	hard sounds (c, k, t, b, p, d)
Present tense	describing events that are currently happening
Pronoun	a word used instead of, and to indicate, a noun, such as 'he' or 'it'
Purpose	the reason for writing or saying something
Repetition	saying a word or idea more than once for effect
Rhetorical question	a question to get someone to think, rather than to get an answer
Second person	addressing your audience, using 'you'
Senses	sight, smell, sound, taste, touch
Sentence	words conveying a statement, question, command or exclamation
Sibilance	repetition of 's' sounds
Simile	a descriptive comparison using 'like' or 'as'
Simple sentence	a sentence that only contains a main clause
Statistic	numerical data
Structure	the way a text is organised and arranged
Subordinate clause	extra information that is added to a main clause
Symbolism	images and symbols that represent ideas
Tense	the form taken by verbs to indicate time
Thematic	linking to subjects or topics
Tone	the emotion of a piece of writing
Topic sentence	an opening sentence that introduces the subject of the paragraph
Triplet	three similar ideas arranged together for effect
Verb	a doing or being word

ACKNOWLEDGEMENTS

The author and publisher are grateful to the copyright holders for permission to use quoted materials and images.

Cover & P1: © Sorbis/Shutterstock.com

All other images are © Hemera/Thinkstock;
© Shutterstock.com and © HarperCollins*Publishers* Ltd

P5: From *Auto da Fay*, by Fay Weldon. Reprinted by permission of HarperCollins*Publishers* Ltd. © Fay Weldon 2002

P6, P7: *From The Kenneth Williams Diaries*, by Russell Davies & Kenneth Williams. Reprinted by permission of HarperCollins *Publishers* Ltd. © Russell Davies and Kenneth Williams 1993

P8, P9, P16: From *Eating for England*, by Nigel Slater. Reprinted by permission of HarperCollins*Publishers* Ltd. © 2007 Nigel Slater

P11, P12, P14: From *Under My Skin*, by Doris Lessing. Reprinted by permission of HarperCollins*Publishers* Ltd. © 1994 Doris Lessing

P11: Letter to Amy Hoare, July 1881, from *Arthur Conan Doyle: A Life in Letters*, by Charles Foley, Daniel Stashower and Jon Lellenberg. Additional approvals courtesy Conan Doyle Estate Ltd.

P12, P13: From *Arthur Conan Doyle: A Life in Letters*, edited by Jon Lellenberg, Daniel Stashower and Charles Foley. Reprinted by permission of HarperCollins*Publishers* Ltd. © Jon Lellenberg, Daniel Stashower and Charles Foley 2007.

P13: From *Mantrapped*, by Fay Weldon. Reprinted by permission of HarperCollins*Publishers* Ltd. © Fay Weldon 2004

P15: 'Five children and an allotment', by Debbie Webber, from *The Guardian*, June 19, 2009. Reprinted by kind permission of Guardian News & Media Ltd.

P19: From *And Then There Were None*, by Agatha Christie. Reprinted by permission of HarperCollins*Publishers* Ltd. © 1939 Agatha Christie [Mallowan]

P21: 'Dressing Up for the Carnival' in *Collected Stories*, by Carol Shields. Reprinted by permission of HarperCollins*Publishers* Ltd. © Carol Shields [Literary Trust] 2004

P26: From *Puffball*, by Fay Weldon. Reprinted by permission of HarperCollins*Publishers* Ltd. © Fay Weldon 1980

P27: From *We Were the Mulvaneys*, by Joyce Carol Oates. Reprinted by permission of HarperCollins*Publishers* Ltd. © Joyce Carol Oates 2001

P29: From *The Rotters' Club*, by Jonathan Coe (Penguin Books, 2002). Copyright © Jonathan Coe, 2001. Reproduced by permission of Penguin Books Ltd.

P30: From *The Falls*, by Joyce Carol Oates. Reprinted by permission of HarperCollins*Publishers* Ltd. © 2004 Joyce Carol Oates

P62: 'First Love' in *Collected Love Poems*, by Brian Patten. Reprinted by permission of HarperCollins*Publishers* Ltd. © Brian Patten 2007

Every effort has been made to trace copyright holders and obtain their permission for the use of copyright material. The author and publisher will gladly receive information enabling them to rectify any error or omission in subsequent editions. All facts are correct at time of going to press.

Published by Letts Educational
An imprint of HarperCollins*Publishers*
1 London Bridge Street
London SE1 9GF

ISBN: 9780008165963

First published 2016

10 9 8 7 6 5 4 3 2 1

© HarperCollins*Publishers* Limited 2016

British Library Cataloguing in Publication Data.
A CIP record of this book is available from the British Library.

Commissioning Editor: Emily Linnett
Author: Ian Kirby
Project Leader: Richard Toms
Project Management and Editorial: Alissa McWhinnie (Q2A Media)
Cover Design: Paul Oates
Inside Concept Design: Ian Wrigley
Text Design and Layout: Q2A Media
Production: Lyndsey Rogers
Printed in China